**Cultural and
Geographical
Exploration**

Indian Tribes of
the Americas

CHRONICLES FROM *NATIONAL GEOGRAPHIC*

Cultural and Geographical Exploration

Ancient Civilizations of the Aztecs and Maya

The Ancient Incas

Australia: The Unique Continent

Building the Panama Canal

Grand Canyon Experiences

Hawaii and the Islands of the Pacific:
A Visit to the South Seas

Indian Tribes of the Americas

Jerusalem and the Holy Land

Lighthouses: Beacons of the Sea

Mysteries of the Sahara

Race for the South Pole—The Antarctic Challenge

Rediscovering Ancient Egypt

Robert E. Peary and the Rush to the North Pole

The Russian People in 1914

Touring America Seventy-Five Years Ago

Touring China Eighty Years Ago

Cultural and Geographical Exploration

Indian Tribes of the Americas

CHRONICLES FROM *NATIONAL GEOGRAPHIC*

Arthur M. Schlesinger, jr.
Senior Consulting Editor

Fred L. Israel
General Editor

CHELSEA HOUSE PUBLISHERS

Philadelphia

CHELSEA HOUSE PUBLISHERS

Editor in Chief Stephen Reginald
Managing Editor James D. Gallagher
Production Manager Pamela Loos
Art Director Sara Davis
Director of Photography Judy L. Hasday
Senior Production Editor LeeAnne Gelletly

The Chelsea House World Wide Web site address is
http://www.chelseahouse.com

First Printing

1 3 5 7 9 8 6 4 2

Library of Congress Cataloging-in-Publication Data

Indian Tribes of the Americas / text provided by
National Geographic Society.
    p. cm. – (Cultural and geographical exploration)
Summary: Articles originally published in "National
Geographic" tell of the archaeological searches for the
ruins of Chaco Canyon, where the Navaho, Zuni, and
Hopi Indian tribes lived, as well as the Pueblo Bonito
expedition.
    ISBN 0-7910-5447-0
    1. Indians of North America—New Mexico—
Chaco Canyon—Antiquities.
    2. Pueblo Bonito Site (N.M.) 3. Chaco Canyon
(N.M.)—Antiquities.
    [1. Indians of North America—New Mexico. 2. Pueblo
Bonito Site (N.M)
    3. Chaco Canyon (N.M)—Antiquities.]
    I. National Geographic Society (U.S.) II. Series.
    E78.N65I52   1999
    978.9'82—dc21   99-28194
                                        CIP

CONTENTS

"THE GREATEST EDUCATIONAL JOURNAL"

When the first *National Geographic* magazine appeared in October 1888, the United States totaled 38 states. Grover Cleveland was President. The nation's population hovered around 60 million. Great Britain's Queen Victoria also ruled as the Empress of India. William II became Kaiser of Germany that year. Czar Alexander III ruled Russia, and the Turkish Empire stretched from the Balkans to the tip of Arabia. To Westerners, the Far East was still a remote and mysterious land. Throughout the world, riding the back of an animal was the principal means of transportation. Unexplored and unmarked places dotted the global map.

On January 13, 1888, thirty-three men—scientists, cartographers, inventors, scholars, and explorers—met in Washington, D.C. They had accepted an invitation from Gardiner Greene Hubbard (1822–1897), the first president of the Bell Telephone Company and a leader in the education of the deaf, to form the National Geographic Society "to increase and diffuse geographic knowledge." One of the assembled group noted that they were the "first explorers of the Grand Canyon and the Yellowstone, those who had carried the American flag farthest north, who had measured the altitude of our famous mountains, traced the windings of our coasts and rivers, determined the distribution of flora and fauna, enlightened us in the customs of the aborigines, and marked out the path of storm and flood." Nine months later, the first issue of *National Geographic* magazine was sent out to 165 charter members. Today, more than a century later, membership has grown to an astounding 11 million in more than 170 nations. Several times that number regularly read the monthly issues of the *National Geographic* magazine.

The first years were difficult ones for the new magazine. The earliest volumes seem dreadfully scientific and quite dull. The articles in Volume I, No. 1 set the tone—W. M. Davis, "Geographic Methods in Geologic Investigation," followed by W. J. McGee, "The Classification of Geographic Forms by Genesis." Issues came out erratically—three in 1889, five in 1890, four in 1891; and two in 1895. In January 1896 "an illustrated monthly" was added to the title. The November issue that year contained a photograph of a half-naked Zulu bride and bridegroom in their wedding finery staring full face into the camera. But, a reader must have wondered what to make of the accompanying text: "These people . . . possess some excellent traits, but are horribly cruel when once they have smelled blood." In hopes of expanding circulation, the Board of Managers offered newsstand copies at $.25 each and began to accept advertising. But the magazine essentially remained unchanged. Circulation rose only slightly.

In January 1898, shortly after Gardiner Greene Hubbard's death, his son-in-law Alexander Graham Bell (1847–1922) agreed to succeed him as the second president of the National Geographic Society. Bell invented the telephone in 1876 and, while pursuing his lifelong goal of improving the lot of the deaf, had turned his amazingly versatile mind to contemplating such varied problems as human flight, air conditioning, and popularizing geography. The society then had about 1,100 members—the magazine was on the edge of bankruptcy. Bell did not want the job. He wrote in his diary, though, that he accepted leadership of the society "in order to save it." "Geography is a fascinating subject and it can be made interesting," he told the board of directors. Bell abandoned the unsuccessful attempt to increase circulation through newsstand sales. "Our journal," he wrote, "should go to members, people who believe in our work and want to help." He understood that the lure for prospective members should be an association with a society that made it possible for the average person to share with kings and scientists the excitement of sending an expedition to a strange land or an explorer to an inaccessible region. This idea, more than any other, has been responsible for the growth of the National Geographic Society and for the popularity of the magazine. "I can well remember," recalled Bell in 1912, "how the idea was laughed at that we should ever reach a membership of ten thousand." That year it had soared to 107,000!

Bell attributed this phenomenal growth, though, to one man who had transformed the *National Geographic* magazine into "the greatest educational journal in the world"—Gilbert H. Grosvenor (1875–1966). Bell had hired Grosvenor, then 24, in 1899 as the National Geographic Society's first full-time employee, "to put some life into the magazine." He personally escorted the new editor, who would become his son-in-law, to the society's headquarters—a small rented room shared with the American Forestry Association on the fifth floor of a building near the U.S. Treasury in downtown Washington. Grosvenor remembered the headquarters "littered with old magazines, newspapers, and a few record books and six enormous boxes crammed with *Geographics* returned by the newsstands." "No desk!" exclaimed Bell. "I'll send you mine." That afternoon, delivery men brought Grosvenor a large walnut rolltop and the new editor began to implement Bell's instructions—to transform the magazine from one of cold geographic fact "expressed in hieroglyphic terms which the layman could not understand into a vehicle for carrying the living, breathing, human-interest truth about this great world of ours to the people." And what did Bell consider appropriate "geographic subjects"? He replied: "The world and all that is in it is our theme."

Grosvenor shared Bell's vision of a great society and magazine that would disseminate geographic knowledge. "I thought of geography in terms of its Greek root: *geographia*—a description of the world," he later wrote. "It thus becomes the most catholic of subjects, universal in appeal, and embracing nations, people, plants, birds, fish. We would never lack interesting subjects." To attract readers, Grosvenor had to change the public attitude toward geography, which he knew was regarded as "one of the dullest of all subjects, something to inflict upon schoolboys and avoid in later life." He wondered why certain books that relied heavily on geographic description remained popular—Charles Darwin's *Voyage of the Beagle*, Richard Dana Jr.'s *Two Years Before the Mast*, and even Herodotus's *History*. Why did readers for generations—and with Herodotus's travels, for 20 centuries—return to these books? What did these volumes, which used so many geographic descriptions, have in common? What was the secret? According to Grosvenor, the answer was that "each was an accurate, eyewitness, firsthand account. Each contained simple straightforward writing—writing that sought to make pictures in the reader's mind."

Gilbert Grosvenor was editor of the *National Geographic* magazine for 55 years, from 1899 until 1954. Each of the 660 issues under his direction had been a highly readable geography textbook. He took Bell's vision and made it a reality. Acclaimed as "Mr. Geography," he discovered the earth anew for himself and for millions around the globe. He charted the dynamic course that the National Geographic Society and its magazine followed for more than half a century. In so doing, he forged an instrument for world education and understanding unique in this or any age. Under his direction, the *National Geographic* magazine grew in circulation from a few hundred copies—he recalled carrying them to the post office on his back—to more than five million at the time of his retirement as editor, enough for a stack 25 miles high.

This Chelsea House series celebrates Grosvenor's first 25 years as editor of the *National Geographic*. "The mind must see before it can believe," said Grosvenor. From the earliest days, he filled the magazine with photographs and established another Geographic principle—to portray people in their natural attire or lack of it. Within his own editorial committee, young Grosvenor encountered the prejudice that photographs had to be "scientific." Too often, this meant dullness. To Grosvenor, every picture and sentence had to be interesting to the layperson. "How could you educate and inform if you lost your audience by boring your readers?" Grosvenor would ask his staff. He persisted and succeeded in making the *National Geographic* magazine reflect this fascinating world.

To the young-in-heart of every age there is magic in the name *National Geographic*. The very words conjure up enchanting images of faraway places, explorers and scientists, sparkling seas and dazzling mountain peaks, strange plants, animals, people, and customs. The small society founded in 1888 "for the increase and diffusion of geographic knowledge" grew, under the guidance of one man, to become a great force for knowledge and understanding. This achievement lies in the genius of Gilbert H. Grosvenor, the architect and master builder of the National Geographic Society and its magazine.

Fred L. Israel
The City College of the City University of New York

INDIAN TRIBES OF THE AMERICAS

Fred L. Israel

Since 1890, the National Geographic Society has financed many scientific expeditions, as well as hundreds of editorial and photographic surveys in all parts of the world. Their results have been presented in the pages of *National Geographic*, month by month, throughout the years. Often such surveys have penetrated remote and little-known regions of the globe, bringing back indispensable contributions to geographic knowledge.

Beginning in 1920, the society sent several expeditions, directed by Neil M. Judd, to make extensive excavations and studies in the Chaco Canyon of northwestern New Mexico. Vast communal dwellings were excavated and interesting relics, including an exquisite turquoise necklace, shed new light on the everyday life of pre-Columbian inhabitants of the southwest. Their ruined buildings, some erected centuries before Columbus reached America, were dated by analyzing the tree rings in the charred and weathered beams. As a result this work was referred to as the society's Tree Ring Expeditions (1923–29). In connection with its work in the Chaco Canyon regions, the Society sent a photographic party into the canyons of northeastern Arizona (1925). This contributed to Neil M. Judd's seminal work *The Material Culture of Pueblo Bonito*, with a preface by Gilbert Grosvenor, published by the Smithsonian Institution.

Judd published five major articles in *National Geographic* between 1922 and 1948. His first article is included in this compilation. It is followed by Fredrick Simpich's account of arbitrary political borders that do not apply to America's native population. This was Simpich's fifth of more than 80 articles that he published in *National Geographic*.

Franklin K. Lane served as Woodrow Wilson's secretary of the interior from 1913 to 1920. His 1915 article for *National Geographic* laments how, according to American law, the Cherokee Indian Nation ceased to exist on July 1, 1914. "The word of the white man has now been made good," wrote a dispirited Lane. "These native and aspiring people have been lifted as American citizens into full fellowship with their civilized conquerers." Lane proceeds to explain America's confusing policies toward the some 300,000 Native Americans then living within the United States. He gives a superb review of America's ambivalence toward the indigenous peoples from the time of the Dawes Act (1887) to the Wilson Administration (1913–21).

The Dawes Act assumed that reservation life perpetrated customs that hindered Indian assimilation into American culture. The act required that Indian tribes would be dissolved, with 160 acres of land given to each family head and 80 acres to each male adult single person. This procedure would occur over a 25-year period. Any reservation land remaining would be open to homesteaders. It is the conclusion of this process as it applied to the Cherokee Indian Nation that Lane refers to in the first paragraphs of his article. Under Lane's tenure as secretary of the interior, the Wilson

Administration favored a contrary policy, an end to assimilation, with power returned to Indian tribes. These ideas eventually were incorporated into the omnibus *Indian Reorganization Act of 1934*.

Henry Pittier's article foreshadowed the uncaring policies that the U.S. government would show toward Indian peoples of Panama as it rushed forward with the completion of the Panama Canal. Pittier was among the first honored by the Society with a lifetime membership, an award reserved for the world's most distinguished geographers.

The series of illustrations on North American Indians found at the end of this volume have been selected from the collection of Edward S. Curtis. In the 1890s, Curtis, a professional photographer, set out to make a photographic record of the Indian tribes. He realized that the habits and character of the few remaining tribes were rapidly disappearing—and that photographs would be of great value to future generations. Curtis continued his work for nine years, assuming all costs.

However, the importance and immensity of the task, as well as the expense, became more and more apparent. In 1906, J. Pierpont Morgan agreed to finance the project through to its conclusion. Eventually, the Smithsonian Institution published 20 volumes of text with 1,500 hundred full-page Curtis photographs, each printed on "the best imported hand-made paper." President Theodore Roosevelt wrote the foreword.

Since 1888, National Geographic has published more than 500 articles dealing with Indians of the Americas. This selection is but a sampling of a unique contribution to the historical record.

A NEW NATIONAL GEOGRAPHIC SOCIETY EXPEDITION

Ruins of Chaco Canyon, New Mexico, Nature-Made Treasure-Chest of Aboriginal American History, to be Excavated and Studied; Work Begins This Month

(With illustrations from photographs by Charles Martin, of the National Geographic Society Reconnaissance Party of 1920)

THE National Geographic Society announces the sending out this summer of an expedition to undertake extensive excavations and studies in the Chaco Canyon of northwestern New Mexico. This expedition hopes to discover the historic secrets of a region which was one of the most densely populated areas in North America before Columbus came, a region where prehistoric peoples lived in vast communal dwellings whose ruins are ranked second to none of ancient times in point of architecture, and whose customs, ceremonies, and name have been engulfed in an oblivion more complete than any other people who left traces comparable to theirs.

Through the findings of this expedition, which begins its work this month (June), the National Geographic Society expects to reveal to its members a shrine of hidden history of their own country.

Both in scientific value of its findings and by adding a new chapter to the progress story of the human race, this project promises to rival such expeditions of The Society as that which dug out the marvelous city of the Andean ancients, Machu Picchu, or that which added to North America's known spots of majesty and seeming magic, the now famous Valley of Ten Thousand Smokes, in the vicinity of Titan Katmai.

A POPULOUS ISLAND IN SEA OF SAND

Chaco Canyon is that segment of the Chaco River which is cut out near the borderland of San Juan and McKinley counties, New Mexico.

PUEBLO BONITO FROM THE NORTHEAST: CHACO CANYON

NORTH WALL OF THE PUEBLO BONITO AS SEEN FROM THE NORTH: CHACO CANYON

Large beams have been torn from the round holes at the top. Today no timber of this size is to be found within forty miles of the canyon. The openings at the ground level have been cut by vandals.

HOPI GIRL OF WALPI (PLACE OF THE NOTCH)

A HOPI "UNIVERSITY" AT WALPI

Garfield's ideal of Mark Hopkins on one end of a log with himself on the other was anticipated by the American Indian, whose tribal leaders are teachers in such primitive but effective agricultural "universities" as this scene discloses.

TWO BEAUTIES OF THE ZUÑI

The Zuñi pottery still is made according to aboriginal methods and patterns. It is as distinctive for its coloring as is the exquisite ware of the Chaco Canyon for its black and white design.

Its sheer, but sometimes crumbling, walls of sandstone rise from its floor anywhere from 100 feet to a height nearly equal to the United States Capitol dome. From their upper ledge stretch semi-desert wastes, making for an isolation which adds another mystery to the bygone metropolis of the canyon's maw: Whence came the lumber to build and whence the water to cultivate the corn, beans, and squash of these aboriginal farms?

To answer questions like these, the expedition not only will include archaeologists, who

NEIL M. JUDD, LEADER OF THE NATIONAL GEOGRAPHIC SOCIETY EXPEDITION,
AND SANTIAGO NARANJO, GOVERNOR OF A TEWA PUEBLO

Having been a member of numerous expeditions sent to study the natural wonders of the Southwest, Mr.. Judd is admirably equipped by experience to undertake the work entrusted to him by the National Geographic Society. He was one of the members of the Utah Expedition and Surveying Party of the General Land Office which in 1909 discovered the Nonnezoshi, greatest of nature's stone bridges (see "The Great Natural Bridges of Utah," in THE GEOGRAPHIC for February, 1910).

PUEBLO BONITO AS SEEN FROM THE CLIFF OF CHACO CANYON, LOOKING TOWARD THE SOUTHEAST

Excavation will outline the structure more clearly and uncover, in addition, the rare treasures of exquisite jet and turquoise ornaments, utensils, and tools of the 1,000 or more aboriginal tenants of this mammoth D-shaped apartment-house, which had an acreage and height comparable to the United States Capitol, disregarding its dome.

will study periods of habitation and the origin of the tribes, but also will have agriculturists and geologists, who hope to patch from a crazy quilt of half-submerged ruins a complete picture of the lives, customs, and culture of these early Americans.

A GIANT CANAL CARVED BY NATURE

From an airplane this gash in the desert surface might resemble a magnified sector of the Panama Canal. Closer inspection would disclose, however, not an expanse of water, but an unwatered canyon, in or bordering which are a dozen huge ruins that look to the casual observer like remains of giant apartment houses, containing hundreds of rooms, with associated temples or sanctuaries known as kivas, and lesser dwellings, the true significance of which is not yet known.

More astounding still, some of these larger structures, such as the Pueblo del Arroyo (arroyo-wash), one of the two ruins upon which The Society's expedition is to concentrate its investigations are built after the familiar E-shaped ground plan of the modern office building, with the addition of a curved wall binding the ends of the E projections and forming inner courts. The other ruin to be studied, Pueblo Bonito (bonito-beautiful), is a D-shaped building, with its curved wall 800 feet long.

Archaeologically this ancient Island of Manhattan, surrounded by a sea of sand, may accurately be described as "a hundred miles from anywhere"; for it is 100 miles north to the cliff dwellings of the Mesa Verde, 100 miles south to the ancient Zuñi towns, and 100 miles west to the ancestral site of the Hopis.

A reconnaissance party dispatched last summer made a report which, when examined by The Society's research committee, bristled with such interesting scientific problems that authorization and appropriation were made for the expedition which begins its work this summer, under the leadership of Neil M. Judd, curator, American Archaeology, U.S. National Museum.

Within an area less than half that of the District of Columbia there are eighteen enormous community houses having from 100 to 800 or more rooms. There also are other structure types, such as the three- to twelve-room dwellings, groups of "talus pueblos" under the wall of the canyon, in the immediate vicinity of the large buildings, and tiny cliff houses and storage cists under the canyon wall itself.

Then there are circular structures, adjacent to both large and small dwellings, and a semi-subterranean home built of mud instead of stone—the last mentioned found by The Geographic's reconnaissance party—which points to possibility of other ruins of greater antiquity that will be invaluable in tracing the development of this aboriginal civilization. The existence of these last mentioned in the Chaco Canyon region had not previously been suspected.

If the major groups were inhabited simultaneously, it is estimated the canyon population could not have been less than 10,000. This Indian city lay in a region so unfriendly that even the nomadic Navajo has not attempted to cultivate it. Hence the question, What has happened there? Did the climate change? Were the surrounding arid wastes once fields of cotton, corn, squash, and beans? Or did these aborigines of northwestern New Mexico have an irrigation system akin to that of the Ifugaos of the Philippines or the rice terraces of China?

Was the American Indian independent of any Nile, toward whose delta such an ingenious people as the Egyptians tended; and did he build apartments no less colossal and of more immediate service than the Egyptian "race of undertakers" constructed for their dead?

One fact is fairly certain, that this people of a period variously placed between the time of Julius Caesar and William the Conqueror had a democratic form of government and elected a governor every year.

To the explorer, the Sherlock Holmes of ancient annals, equipped with pick and shovel, even a cursory inspection reveals clues that point to the recovery of buried treasure of history. For example, attention was attracted by masonry reinforced by timbers beneath the precipitous rocks that frown over the Pueblo Bonito. This represents a naive effort to support a huge mass of solid rock weighing thousands of tons which threatened to topple on the great building beneath. This child-like engineering experiment was surprising, in view of the architectural skill disclosed in the construction of buildings which are superior in masonry to any other aboriginal structures in the United States.

The Society's reconnaissance party examined and reported upon the availability of 16 of

TINY WARRIORS OF THE "PEACEFUL PEOPLE": ARIZONA

These Hopi youngsters are "children of the sun" in a double sense. They are dedicated to that luminary deity by their parents, and are completely exposed to its penetrating desert rays until they are well into their teens. As their name signifies, the Hopi Indians are pacific; but they are far from being pacifists. Their "standing army" consists of a clan in which every mother raises her son to be a warrior; just as certain other clans are entrusted with the perpetuation of the Snake Dance and similar customs. The extinct Chaco Canyon pueblo people (see "A New National Geographic Society Expedition," pages 1 to 18) may have had an even more complex social organization, for they dwelt in apartment-houses compared to which many pueblo dwellings are but groups of cottages.

CLIFF PALACE: MESA VERDE

This most celebrated of Mesa Verde ruins is an example of a pueblo type in contrast to that of Bonito. The forgotten people of the Chaco found in canyon depths a refuge which the Mesa Verde dwellers utilized a cliff to attain. Recently a subterranean entrance was discovered to this "palace," of 200 rooms.

the canyon's 19 major ruins. The Pueblo Bonito and the Pueblo del Arroyo were selected as promising the richest rewards. These two ruins lie in the very heart of the Chaco Canyon National Monument.

Pueblo Bonito has been called the foremost prehistoric ruin in the United States. It is the largest of the ruins, the most complex in design, the most impressive. It seems to tell most clearly the unwritten story of the forgotten people who once dwelt within its silent walls. It covers an area approximately that of the United States Capitol. Its 800 rooms probably sheltered from 1,000 to 1,200 souls.

These mysterious tenants tilled the soil of the broad, level canyon floor; they hunted deer and antelope on the mesas overlooking the valley; they probably waged war on the Navajo, the Philistines who pressed upon them from the north.

RUINS ARE DEPOSIT VAULTS OF CERAMIC TREASURES

Already ceramic remains of rare artistry have been taken from Pueblo Bonito, exquisite ornaments of jet and turquoise mosaic, tools and utensils of bone, stone, and wood. Tons of

WHERE NATURE UPSET HER PAINT-POT: CANYON DE CHELLY

Bright red sandstone cliffs, piercing the sky to heights ranging between that of the Washington Monument and of the Eiffel Tower, sheltered a prehistoric people, probably of the same general period as those of Chaco Canyon. This most brilliantly colored of all the canyons of the Southwest lies in the heart of the Navajo Desert, northeastern Arizona.

earth and stone have been removed in search of material. Yet the great ruin still guards priceless secrets. The architecture remains to be studied and further evidence of the pursuits of its people needs to be found and interpreted.

Less than a city block west of Pueblo Bonito is Pueblo del Arroyo, occupying a perilous position, as indicated by its name; for the wash, or arroyo, which passes the structure threatens to cut away the bank upon which the ruin is sit-

uated. The pueblo virtually is virgin soil for the investigator. It probably stood four stories high. The upper story is gone, the first is buried, leaving only the second and third exposed.

It possesses characteristics that make all the ruins noteworthy and one, in addition, of paramount importance. Beneath the pueblo, exposed only by the caving of the arroyo bank, is a dwelling of the "small-house" type noted above. It is considered that two periods of occupancy at one site, each with its distinctive remains, offers

AN OLD WAR CAPTAIN OF LAGUNA PUEBLO, NEW MEXICO

The bow and arrow today are relics of bitter tribal wars of long ago. A more potent mace is a cane, prized by many council chiefs, who hold this symbol of prestige because of a visit to the "Great White Father" in Washington. Some of these canes have been handed down from patriarchs who made the cross-continent journey during Lincoln's administration.

an unparalleled opportunity for study of culture sequence. So far as is known, this is the only instance in Chaco Canyon where such superposition occurs. The fortunate proximity of Pueblo del Arroyo and Pueblo Bonito affords one

advantage to the expedition in a region where many handicaps must be overcome.

Geographically the Chaco Canyon ruins have a special interest. They denote admirably the exceptional characteristics that result from

HOPI POTTERS OF ARIZONA ENGAGED IN AN ART THAT SURVIVES THE CENTURIES

Compared with these Indian workers of 1921, Cape Cod fishermen are followers of an infant American industry. Ceramics have more than an aesthetic significance. Pottery making, for example, is indicative of a pueblo people, for the ware is too fragile for nomad use.

an exceptional environment. Being a people hemmed in by natural barriers, their area of activity was restricted.

They were able to meet their material needs by expending only a fraction of their energy.

Hence the surplus found expression in religious ritual, attested by the great ceremonial chambers; in architectural monuments, as did that of the European cathedral builders of the Middle Ages; and in ceramics, which flourished there as never

EL RITO DE LES FRIJOLES (LITTLE CANYON OF THE BEANS): NEW MEXICO

The honeycomb circlet in the foreground is the pueblo ruin of Tyuonyi. This photograph was taken from the top of a cliff along whose base for three miles stretches a series of "talus pueblos," a type of dwelling also found in Chaco Canyon (see text, page 7).

CANYON DE CHELLY MONUMENT: ARIZONA

In the shadow at the base to the right a cliff dwelling was found. On a ledge just above is a man, whose form is a tiny speck against this lone sentinel among the fantastic "backdrops" of multi-hued canyon walls.

"BRACED-UP" CLIFF AT PUEBLO BONITO, CHACO CANYON

The scattered stones at the bottom of this leaning tower of Chaco are an enigma. They represent a naïve effort to prop up a massive cube of solid rock on the part of these aboriginal engineers, who exhibited contrasting skill and acumen in the construction of Pueblo Bonito, to the left (see also text, page 7).

before or since, for the black and white ware of the Chaco Canyon has been cited as marking the high point of this art in the Southwest.

Other departments of science may be expected to profit by results of the Chaco Canyon investigations. The excavations and repairs of the ruins, their architecture and masonry, fall under the head of archaeology. What is learned of their builders, where they came from, how long they stayed in the canyon, and where they went are questions related to ethnology.

CANYON DEL MUERTO, A BRANCH OF CANYON DE CHELLY: ARIZONA

Cliff dwellings abound on nearly every ledge. It is not strange that peoples living in such an environment should conceive man to have emerged from a vent in the earth's surface.

The Chaco Canyon is a desert today, unwatered except by floods in the rainy season. The geologist must be relied upon to describe conditions of water supply and crops when the great houses were occupied. Specialists in desert flora must cooperate with the geologist in an effort to picture the economic life of these ancients. Only by the combined findings of these various experts can it be determined whether the inhabitants left because natural changes threatened their food supply, or whether falling cliff masses impressed their superstitious minds as being omens of evil.

EVENING EFFECT: WALPI, ARIZONA

Like the people of San Marino, who climbed a mountain to live in liberty and serenity, the Hopi, self-styled "People of Peace," took refuge in the cliffs of northeastern Arizona to avoid constant warring with cruder tribes. Walpi is on the summit of a sheer cliff.

Being within the Chaco Canyon National Monument, the Pueblo Bonito and Pueblo del Arroyo ruins are reserved and protected for the American people. The National Geographic Society's investigations, made possible under a permit granted by the Secretary of the Interior, therefore constitute a gift to the public.

The excavations, at the expense of The Society, should solve many of the problems now apparent. Repairs will prevent rapid disintegration of the walls and insure longer life to the ruins.

THE GREAT KIVA OF PUEBLO BONITO, WITH ITS SURROUNDING ROOMS, VIEWED FROM THE NORTH CLIFF (SEE TEXT ON OPPOSITE PAGE)

This was the most important council chamber or ceremonial room of the Bonitians. The small hollowed square of masonry in the center of the room was the fireplace.

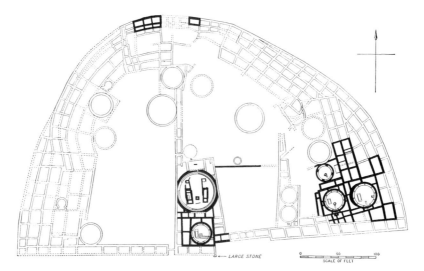

A DIAGRAM OF PUEBLO BONITO: THE BLACK LINES SHOW THE PORTION OF THE RUIN EXCAVATED BY THE NATIONAL GEOGRAPHIC SOCIETY'S EXPEDITION OF 1921

During the coming summer the 1922 expedition will continue its work on the ruins at the right, working in a northwesterly direction.

THE PUEBLO BONITO EXPEDITION OF THE NATIONAL GEOGRAPHIC SOCIETY

By NEIL M. JUDD
Leader of the National Geographic Society's Expedition of 1921 and 1922

PUEBLO BONITO is a pre-Columbian village, now in ruins, situated in northwestern New Mexico. Its exact age is unknown, but there is an increasing hope that this will be closely approximated before our studies have been completed.

We might, I believe, assume with some degree of certainty that the village was occupied 1,000 years ago.

I do not mean to say that Pueblo Bonito was erected or that it was abandoned, in the year 922 A.D. My thought is that if it had been possible for us to look down from the cliffs say 800 or 1,200 years ago, it is likely we should have seen happy children at play on the housetops and their elders busy with varied activities in and about the village.

Pueblo Bonito is a colossal apartment-house, not the first of its kind, but one of the largest and best known at that early period. Its equipment, its furniture, is a bit out of date, to be sure, but many a city dweller of today would welcome the freedom of its spacious rooms (see diagram, page 18).

This aboriginal village or pre-Columbian apartment hotel was a whole community in itself, since it covered a little more than three acres and sheltered between 1,200 and 1,500 individuals. Roughly speaking, its foundations were approximately equal to those of the United States Capitol.

There were more than 300 rooms on its ground floor; its outer walls were four perhaps five, stories high. Portions of fourth-story walls still stand. Its houses were terraced upward from two inner plazas or courts, like the magnified seats of an amphitheater.

The modern pueblo of Acoma, southwest of Albuquerque, New Mexico, possesses several features closely paralleling those of Pueblo Bonito. Its houses are in long rows, with a high wall on one side, unbroken except for small ventilators, and, opposite, stepped houses overlooking the plazas. Acoma is the oldest continuously inhabited settlement in the United States; its population has been estimated at between 1,000 and 2,000 when the Spaniards first attacked it, in 1540 (see photograph, page 20).

CAMP OF THE NATIONAL GEOGRAPHIC SOCIETY'S 1921 PUEBLO BONITO EXPEDITION

THE MODERN PUEBLO OF ACOMA CROWNING A ROCK FORMATION
SOUTHWEST OF ALBUQUERQUE, NEW MEXICO

This, the oldest continuously inhabited pueblo in the United States, possesses several features closely paralleling those of Pueblo Bonito (see text, page 19).

THE SOUTHEAST SECTION OF PUEBLO BONITO
(NORTHWESTERN NEW MEXICO), SHOWING PART OF THE ROOMS EXCAVATED
BY THE NATIONAL GEOGRAPHIC SOCIETY'S 1921 EXPEDITION

The partially razed camp of the 1921 expedition is seen in the upper right-hand corner. The 1922 expedition will leave Washington in a few weeks to pursue its work of excavation and exploration. The vast ruins were occupied a thousand years ago by perhaps 1,200 or 1,500 individuals (see text, page 19).

Our initial explorations, conducted during the summer of 1921, afford a reasonably accurate view of Pueblo Bonito. The building is semicircular. It is 310 feet north and south; its south face is 518 feet long. If stood on end, this wall would reach to the windows of the Washington Monument.

The twenty or more circular kivas (a kiva was both a council chamber and a religious sanctuary) border the two open spaces where

THE HOPI VILLAGE OF WALPI, WHOSE TERRACED
HOUSES STAND OUT AGAINST THE BLUE ARIZONA SKY

This is the most picturesque of the Hopi towns, and some of the clans of this tribe of Indians are known to have migrated from cliff dwellings such as those found in Mesa Verde, Colorado. The Zuñi Indians say the Hopi people built the great houses of Chaco Canyon (see text, page 27).

PERHAPS AMONG THE TRADITIONS OF HIS PEOPLE, THE
SOLUTION OF THE MYSTERY OF PUEBLO BONITO WILL BE FOUND

This Zuñi boy may be a descendant of the aboriginal artisans who quarried the stone and mixed the mud that
went into the towering walls of Pueblo Bonito (see text, page 19).

public ceremonies were enacted. The clustered
dwellings overlooking these courts furnished
seats for gathered spectators, just as the housetops of Oraibi are now utilized during the
Snake Dance and other native dramas.

The shaded sections of the diagram on
page 18 mark most of the rooms excavated last
summer, but tests made elsewhere disclosed
buried structures not shown on this plan.

THE BONITIANS USED
THREE TYPES OF MASONRY

One of the most important results of our
first season's work was identification of three
distinct types of masonry employed in construction of the pueblo.

In the north and northwest sections of
the ruin, dwellings with very crude stonework

THREE TYPES OF PUEBLO BONITO MASONRY

Each of the sections photographed is two feet square. Crude stonework (left) is found in the oldest portion of the ruin. The middle picture shows a second type in which sandstone blocks, rubbed smooth on the face, and small, thin chips are characteristic. The latest masonry (right) consists of rather uniform fragments of laminate sandstone laid close together (see text, pages 23–24).

are found. These houses formed the nucleus of Pueblo Bonito; their builders possessed a culture cruder and less artistic than that of the peoples who came later to join with them and who were largely responsible, we may safely assume, in the development of the great community whose shattered walls first attracted our attention and now command our admiration.

The outline of this more primitive settlement has not been wholly traced, owing to the fact that it was partially destroyed and built over as newer buildings were erected.

The illustration on this page shows the three principal types of masonry—the oldest, the latest, and the intermediate.

Whenever one of the old Bonitians got a new idea, he set about its realization, even if this meant destruction of the house he had erected with infinite labor. Beneath a large

majority of the 40-odd rooms excavated during the summer of 1921 we found the razed walls of still older houses.

The excellent example of the second type of masonry shows blocks of friable sandstone rubbed smooth on the face, laid in adobe mud, and chinked with innumerable small chips.

Walls of the later period are of laminate sandstone, laid close together and frequently with larger blocks placed to form decorative bands.

These variations in masonry can mean only this: Irresistible influences were at work, asserting their supremacy. But whether these influences represent merely local developments or cultural phases introduced by newcomers is a problem we have yet to solve. We know that peoples from other regions came to dwell at Pueblo Bonito, for we have found numerous examples of their characteristic arts.

DIFFICULTIES AND REWARDS IN PUEBLO BONITO RESEARCH

This work of exploration, this digging into deep rooms, this ferreting out of hidden facts, has its difficulties and its rewards.

The chief recompense is the satisfaction one derives from adding a few sentences to the world's history, in contributing even a short paragraph to the story of human progress. There is an immeasurable joy in starting work on a gigantic rock pile—the accumulation of fallen walls and centuries of windblown sand—and finding, after a few hours' labor, a whole series of ancient dwellings unfolding itself.

Fragments of information, constantly being uncovered, hold one to the task. Teams can be used upon occasion, where the amount of earth to be removed exceeds the quantity of stone, but difficulties increase in proportion to depth, and the uninitiated can scarcely realize the problem of clearing deep rooms beneath interlocked and, often, insecure walls.

WAR CLOUDS OFTEN DISSIPATED WITH CANDY

Early spring months in desert canyons of the Southwest are notorious for their sand-storms, and our camp was exposed to all the winds that blew, no hidden corner being safe from permeating dust clouds. In direct contrast, midsummer brings the rainy season, when everything, even one's sense of humor, gets wet and soggy.

The sandstorms were a daily torment throughout the greater portion of the summer.

It was a weird sight indeed to see a cloud of flour-like sand rolling over a distant cliff and up the canyon on the very heels of a saturating shower. Nothing escaped this dust; it found a way beneath watch crystals, into locked trunks, and, worst of all, into food served by an incomparable cook.

During the first busy weeks in camp and before our tardy tents arrived, sand showered down on piles of equipment like a fog of pumice thrown out by that greatest spewer of all, old Katmai.* For partial protection the camp stove was dragged to a neglected dugout fresh with the unmistakable odor of Navaho goats; then a rude screen was raised, and still later the front of the shed was completely closed.

Happily, the intensity of these periodic storms decreased as the season advanced, but the smell and the taste of them remained to the very end.

Early and late, each day ushers in its own problems in the work of excavation, and there is also the ever-threatening possibility that one or more amiable-looking Indians will flare up over some imagined injustice, causing temporary mutiny in the ranks. War clouds have been dissipated more than once with a handful of cheap candy or a five-cent bag of imitation tobacco. I am a firm believer in the efficacy of the lowly gumdrop and the pipe of peace.

And then there is the mother-in-law question. I suppose no previous expedition of the National Geographic Society has been made the victim of the famous mother-in-law joke; but the Navaho have a belief that a man becomes blind if he looks upon his wife's mother. The tradition has its obvious advantages and its disadvantages. If during the working day the mother-in-law of one of our Navaho men happened to pass, the latter abruptly turned his

---

* See accounts of Mt. Katmai and the Valley of Ten Thousand Smokes in the NATIONAL GEOGRAPHIC MAGAZINE for February, 1913, January, 1917, February, 1918, and September, 1921.

HE DUPLICATES PREHISTORIC MASONRY

Jack Lavery was intrusted with the important task of repairing the shattered walls of Pueblo Bonito. His genial smile and his skill in imitating accurately the handiwork of ancient artisans won him the Zuñi name "Enote Nahme"—Prehistoric Grandfather.

back or dropped his shovel and pulled his shirt over his head simulating a hiding ostrich, until she had disappeared.

THE ANCIENT BONITIANS
WERE TRUE NEIGHBORS

The ancient Bonitians were agriculturists by choice—permanent habitations were erected only by sedentary agriculturally inclined peoples—and yet a portion of their food supply was obtained by hunting the deer, the antelope, and the wild turkey.

They were true neighbors to each other and had developed the community spirit to a high degree. Locked doors were unknown in Pueblo Bonito. As an example of the cooperative spirit which prevailed, I would cite the skeleton of a mule deer, fragments of which were found in a dozen different rooms. The animal had been killed by one or more hunters and its flesh distributed among the immediate neighbors.

Construction of Pueblo Bonito was a community enterprise. Gathering the stone, bringing mud and water, and transporting the huge beams that roofed the dwellings were tasks shared by its inhabitants.

The garden plots tended by the menfolk were considered town property; the whole village united in planting and harvesting the principal food crops. Corn, beans, and squash were raised, but the Bonitians depended, also, upon seeds from the wild grasses which carpeted their sandy mesas.

The village was governed by regularly chosen representatives, who met in the kivas and transacted their business under protection of supernatural beings.

PUEBLO MYTHOLOGY MAY HELP TO SOLVE MYSTERY OF BONITIANS

We do not know where the original settlers came from; their origin has not yet been traced definitely. Research will determine this in time; but there is another source of information to be drawn upon. I refer to the mythology of inhabited Pueblo villages in New Mexico and Arizona.

The modern pueblos, as we know them, are made up largely of previously unrelated groups, brought together for common defense against ancient enemies and, later, against the Spanish conquerors of the 16th and 17th centuries.

During recent excavations at Hawikuh, one of Coronado's "Seven Cities of Cibola," remains were found of a still older ruin, in which certain features are not unlike those in Chaco Canyon pueblos.

Acoma, on its lofty pedestal, may hold an important clue for us. It is the oldest inhabited village in the United States, and I have already mentioned certain architectural similarities between its dwellings and those of Pueblo Bonito.

It may be that our solution will be found in Walpi, most picturesque of the Hopi towns (see page 22). My Zuñi workmen, perhaps in an effort to shield their own traditions, expressed the belief that Hopi peoples had built the great houses of Chaco Canyon. There may or may not be a basis for this assertion, but some of the Hopi clans are known to have migrated from cliff-dwellings in the San Juan drainage, among which those of the Mesa Verde stand supreme. The characteristic pottery of this region has been found among the later dwellings at Pueblo Bonito.

The Navaho possess a questionable myth that their ancestors attacked Pueblo Bonito, driving out its inhabitants, who fled to Zuñi. Native historians may hold the key to our problem, but only time and an absolute confidence in a friendly questioner will separate it and them. Who knows if the Zuñi boy (shown on page 23) is a descendant of the aboriginal artisans who quarried the stone and mixed the mud that went into the towering walls of Pueblo Bonito?

On long winter evenings, in modern pueblos, the boys gather around the old men, bask in the warmth of an open fire, and draw forth tales of "the people who used to be." These stories form the unwritten histories of various groups; they trace clan migrations from ancestral homes; they hold the heart-burnings of peaceful village folk, exiled by threatenig blows from an enemy tomahawk.

How easy it would all be if we possessed the far-seeing eye of tribal heroes; if we could

IN THE "LITTLE CANYON OF THE BEANS"

The canyon is located northwest of Santa Fé, New Mexico, within easy automobile distance, and is visited by many tourists. Ancient peoples of this valley carved with stone implements small rooms called "cavate lodges" in the sheer cliffs of tufa, and were therefore under no compulsion to construct elaborate community houses such as are to be found at Pueblo Bonito.

CAUGHT IN THE QUICKSANDS

The expedition car was caught in Chaco Canyon quicksands one Sunday afternoon when on exploration duty, and this photograph was taken while waiting for an Indian runner to fetch help. After six hours' strenuous work the machine was rescued through the united efforts of ten men, a team of horses, and a second truck; once on firm ground, it returned to camp (see illustration, page 20) under its own power.

only picture the scenes that have been witnessed from the ancient watch-tower which still stands sentinel over the ruins of Pueblo Bonito.

Once we possess the outlines of such myths as may still exist, the cultural objects now deeply buried beneath the crumbling walls of the Beautiful Village will take on a new meaning and a new value. With these objects we can retrieve the unwritten records of Pueblo Bonito and establish for this greatest of all our pre-Columbian ruins in the United States its true relationship to the human history of the New World.

ALONG OUR SIDE OF
THE MEXICAN BORDER

By Frederick Simpich

Fomerly American Consul at Nogales, Mexico, Author of "Where Adam and Eve Lived,"
"Mystic Nedjef, the Shia Mecca," "The Rise of the New Arab Nation," etc.

THE Mexican border! What a frequent phrase! How it hints at turmoil and intrigue, at wild night rides by cavalry patrols, at gunrunners and smugglers! How suggestive it is, too, of girls in red skirts and *mantillas*, peddling *tamales* and *dulces*; of Mexican women washing clothes, babies, and dishes in irrigation ditches; of burros, hens, and pigs foraging about adobe doorways!

For years our papers have run news stories under border town date-lines, telling of turbulence and strife, of adventure, romance, and intrigue. Hardly a week passes but a front-page story "breaks" somewhere on the Mexican border. No region in all North America is more frequently mentioned or more widely misunderstood, perhaps, as regards places,* routes,

distances, and the habits and customs of its people.

Now a boundary, they used to tell us at school, is an imaginary line between two countries. But in various jails hard by this long line of muddy water and stone obelisks that marks where the U.S.A. quits and Mexico begins, there are always a few tardy fugitives who deny that this line is "imaginary." It unites us with Mexico, or separates us from it, they say, depending on the humor of border sheriffs at particular moments.

At Nogales they tell of a fugitive from American justice, hard pressed by the Yankee police, who fled and fell sprawling fairly across this line—his head and shoulders in Mexico, the rest of his body in Arizona. Frantically his waiting Mexican friends grabbed him by hair and hands, seeking to drag him over to safety.

But a pursuing constable dropped heavily on the fugitive's feet, with a pistol against the American part of his anatomy, and bawled such ominous threats that the runaway squirmed hastily home again. More than one border bad

---

*A common cause of geographic confusion is the large number of towns in our Southwest which bear Spanish names, and the frequent recurrence of these identical town names in Mexico. Names like Santa Cruz, Del Rio, Casa Grande, etc., occur on both sides of the line. "Alamos" are found by the dozen; likewise "San Juans."

A UNIT IN THE STREET RAILWAY TRANSPORTATION
SERVICE OF A MEXICAN BORDER CITY

This type of street-car may seem obsolete to the individual accustomed to the modern electric line, but less than a quarter of a century ago the horse-car was in use in Washington, D.C., and it disappeared from the cross-streets of New York City less than a decade ago.

man "bit the dust" because he didn't know just where this line was or didn't reach it in time.

In other ways the social cleavage of this border is sharp and startling. It cuts us off abruptly from another people, showing an odd, interesting "cross-section" of diverse civilizations, proving again what the Roman said about races of men differing in manners and habits, in standards and traditions.

Nor are all the people along this line either Yankees or Mexicans. Thousands of Chinese are settled here, on the Mexican side; and Turks and Japanese, and twenty Indian tribes speaking twenty of the babel of tongues heard in Mexico.

IT'S A LONG, CROOKED LINE

Thousands of settlers migrate to this border-land each year, losing themselves in the vast, hazy-blue stretches of its open country; but they are Americans all, mostly from the Middle West and the South. The hordes of Finns, Slavs, and Neapolitans that pour into our Atlantic ports never get this far; they stop in the manufacturing centers of the East. In Texas and California, of course, native-born generations are found; in the newer States of Arizona and New Mexico most of the residents (barring children) have come from other States.

Adventurous, colorful, and full of contrasts as it is, the 1,800-mile trip along this crooked, historic line is rough and difficult and has been made by few people.

Some of the wildest and least known regions of our country are piled up against this border. Ask any doughboy, of the many, many thousands who have done a "hitch" on the Mexican border, what he thinks, for instance, of Ajo or the Yuma sector (see map, page 45).

From the Gulf up to El Paso, along the Texas frontier, the Rio Grande forms the boundary between the United States and Mexico; thence to the Pacific coast the line is marked by stone or iron monuments (save a short break at the Colorado), so set that one is supposed to be visible from another. By this plan a soldier, miner, or cowman (yes, and a smuggler, too) can always tell which side of the line he is on; or, if wholly lost and he comes suddenly on a monument, he can soon get oriented.

The Rio Grande part of this border has caused both Uncle Sam and Mexico much work and mental anguish. During bad floods the line as formed by the river squirms around in so astonishing and lively a manner that what is Mexican soil one day may be in Texas the next, and *vice versa*.

Then, too, there is the ever-recurring problem of dividing the waters of the river for irrigating purposes. Around such places as Laredo, Texas, this situation affords many an acrimonious international argument, especially during the low-water period in the summer.

Sometimes the Texans open their sluices and threaten the ruin of the little *fincas* on the opposite bank; then the Mexican recalls the time when the grand Mexican State of Coahuila extended westward to the Pacific Ocean and almost up to Kansas City, Missouri.

When there is a heavy snowfall in the mountains of New Mexico and Colorado, the spring freshets fill the Rio Grande with a flood that brooks no turning; weirs, gates, and bridges are swept away, the river banks and the adjacent farms are often submerged, and the nagging contestants for the river's midsummer favors are forced to flee to the highlands.

RAILROADS THAT CUT THE BORDER

Railroads cut this long border line at Brownsville, Laredo, Eagle Pass, and El Paso, Texas; at Douglas, Naco, and Nogales, in Arizona, and at Calexico and Tia Juana, in California. Only four of these railroads, however, are main lines of through traffic that penetrate the interior of Mexico; these start at Laredo, Eagle Pass, El Paso, and Nogales.

Mexico itself, area considered, has comparatively few miles of railroad, and there is no line traversing its northern frontier east and west, like our Southern Pacific, which practically parallels most of our southern border.

ALONG THE TEXAN FRONTIER

You visualize the bigness of Texas when you look at the length of its side that borders on Mexico. It has been said that "if you should tip the State up and drop it north, like a flapjack, it would fall on St. Paul; tip it east and it would splash in the Atlantic; south, it would blot out most of Mexico." Its area is more than double that of the British Isles.

You realize its emptiness, too, when you travel through some of its border regions, where the population is less than two people per square mile. If all the people in the United States were put in Texas, it would still be

AN AMERICAN ARMY ESCORT ACTING AS A CONVOY
FOR SUPPLIES ALONG THE MEXICAN BORDER

The scene is that of a typical alkali plain, where only snakes and cacti thrive, and where the dust is so penetrating that it will find its way into the watch in one's pocket. Before railways were built in the southern republic, a Mexican president characterized this desert as his country's strongest defense against invasion.

scarcely more than two thirds as crowded as England.

No section of the border has seen so much of adventure, tragedy, and turbulent activity as Texas. The flags of France, Spain, and Mexico have waved over it; for a time it flew its own Lone Star and also the Confederate flag.

"If I owned Hades and Texas, I'd rent Texas and live in the other place," Phil Sheridan said when, as a young lieutenant, he stood "The Watch on the Rio Grande," way back in the 1850's. But since then Texas, like Arizona, has cast out its devils. It was absolutely "bone dry" long before July 1, 1919; today only the police can "tote" guns; poker is taboo, and even bridge for a cent a point may land you in the "hoose gow"—Texas for *juzgado* (jail).

In Brownsville you hear more Spanish than English, because most of the 8,000 people who live there are Mexicans. Until the railroad

came, a few years ago, this remote, isolated region was practically unknown to Americans at large. It is still a wild, thinly populated, stockgrowing district: The natives plow and haul largely with ox-teams. As one writer said "Even if Texas has been occupied by white men for four centuries, it is still somewhat new in spots—and big spots at that."

Zachary Taylor built a fort in 1846 hard by this same Brownsville. When his men got into a shooting scrape with Mexican soldiers from Matamoras they started the Mexican War, and the Rio Grande became the boundary between the two republics.

Up the river from Brownsville lies Laredo, the most important border town in south Texas, even if an old map does call this vicinity "a wilderness filled with wild horses." Here you may still see the ruins of old stone houses and tanks built by Spanish planters generations ago.

Laredo staged many dramatic events in the stirring annals of Texas. Today, however, the people have turned from romance to onions. They shipped 2,500 carloads in one season.

Until the International and Great Northern Railway extended its line from San Antonio, Laredo also was shut off from the rest of Texas; now it is the main port of entry for traffic with Mexico City, over the Mexican National Railway.

Eagle Pass, on up the Rio Grande, was a favorite camping spot for the California gold-hunters in 1849. Yankee freighters from St. Louis, too, used to drive through here for Chihuahua and Durango.

Worn, weather-beaten carretas, clumsy carts with solid wood wheels sawn from huge logs and built wholly without nails or spikes, are occasionally seen even now, abandoned in some brush-grown corral, reminding you of the slow, tedious transportation of early days, when it took a year to get freight from New York to Durango.

Now a branch of the Southern Pacific strikes the border at Eagle Pass, and from the Mexican town of Piedras Negras (Black Rocks), just opposite, a line of the Mexican National runs south into one of Mexico's most fertile regions. This gives Eagle Pass a brisk trade.

No spot on the whole border affords more of impressive grandeur than the region about the mouth of the Pecos. This yellow, turbulent stream roars into the Rio Grande near the town of Del Rio, foaming along the bottom of a steep-walled canyon worn hundreds of feet deep in the solid rock. The Southern Pacific Railway crosses this canyon, near the border, on one of the greatest steel trestles ever built.

At the old Fort at Camp Verde, north of Uvalde, is a relic of one of the oddest experiments ever made by our government. It is an Arab *khan*, in ruins now, but in its time an exact replica of the rectangular adobe caravansaries built along such caravan trails as that from Bagdad to Teheran. Back in 1856, when Jefferson Davis was Secretary of War and the famous experiment was made with camels for army transport use between Texas and California, this *khan* was built.*

As you follow the border west, oaks, pines, and underbrush decrease, aridity increases, and cacti lift their thorny heads. Cattle, goats, and sheep are pastured in large numbers; but, except for irrigated areas along the river, the country is thinly settled and undeveloped. Border counties like Brewster, Presidio, and El Paso are of amazing area—larger than some of our small eastern States. Windmills are everywhere—"big electric fans to keep the cattle cool," a waggish cowboy once explained to a London tenderfoot.

El Paso ("The Pass"), great border mart of west Texas, is set on the edge of a rich stretch of the Rio Grande Valley. It stands at the point of intersection of two old highways, the first channels of traffic established by white men in America.

A popular automobile trail to the Pacific coast now runs this way. Coronado, pathfinder

---

*Camel transportation along the Mexican border was undertaken by the government with two herds, totaling about 75 animals, including a few two-humped Bactrian males, imported for breeding purposes. Six Arabs and a Bedouin camel doctor came along, from Smyrna to Texas. Lieutenant Edward F. Beale, under orders to establish a military road from San Antonio to California, used these camels in transport work. The camels were given a thorough test, and in Beale's report he spoke in highest terms of their work; but army horses and pack-mules were stampeded: obstinate mule-skinners refused to handle "circus animals"; so finally the camels were disposed of. Most of them were sold to zoölogical parks, but a few either got away or were turned loose on the desert. Prospectors, enraged when these ungainly brutes terrified their pack-mules, used to shoot them on sight. Even now, once in a while a desert rat drifts into Yuma or Gila Bend and vows he's seen a wild camel on the desert. Maybe he did, but nobody believes him.

for border tourists, blazed the way in 1540, on his march to Santa Fe, and long ago El Paso was the headquarters for the Spanish Government in this part of America.

THE ONLY LARGE CITY BETWEEN SAN ANTONIO AND LOS ANGELES

El Paso is the only large city from "San Antone" to Los Angeles, a ride of 1,500 dry, dusty miles. It is well served by both American and Mexican railways, and its merchants buy and sell goods for hundreds of miles below the Rio Grande. Despite the arid country about it and its occasional blinding dust-storms, its climate is exceptionally good, owing to high elevation.

Summer showers afford a rainfall of about 10 inches. Soil is fertile in the valleys cutting the adjacent plateau country, and good crops are grown wherever ample irrigation is possible.

The largest irrigation reservoir anywhere is the great Elephant Butte dam, which stores more water than the world-famous Assuan dam on the Nile. This big dam, built in the Rio Grande above El Paso, at a point in New Mexico, holds water enough, we are told, "to fill a standpipe 11 feet in diameter reaching from El Paso to the moon, or to cover Massachusetts to a depth of six inches!" Enough water can be stored to last through four dry seasons and to irrigate 300 square miles; but by an international agreement a part of the water goes to irrigate land in Mexico.

Fort Bliss, one of our largest permanent military barracks, is built just outside El Paso.

JUAREZ, A CITY KNOWN CHIEFLY FOR ITS BATTLES AND GAY AMERICAN TOURISTS

Juarez, El Paso's sister city across the Rio Grande, like most Mexican border towns, is known chiefly because of its pitched battles and its bizarre methods of entertaining sporty American visitors. Whatever it enjoys of life and prosperity it draws from Yankee tourist patronage.

A wooden bridge spans the river here, and El Paso street-cars loop over into Mexico, when the looping is safe.

Thousands of tourists swarm across this bridge each year to play the races, have a fling at keno or chuck-a-luck, or to mail bullfight or *ballerina* picture postals to the home folks to show that the writer has been "gay, blithe, and devilish in foreign parts."

It is a typical Mexican frontier town of squat, one-story adobe houses (plastered and painted light blue or pink), of *tiendas*, plazas, casinos, bull rings, Chinese restaurants, curio stores, and often a few lurking American derelicts waiting here till the sheriffs in their home towns are dead.

Like the natives of Nogales, Agua Prieta, and Naco, most of the inhabitants of Juarez make a living by working in the adjacent American border town—swarming to the American side, carrying babies and bundles, when the rebel alarm is raised. From Juarez, Mexican railways lead off south, connecting with most important interior cities.

ONLY EIGHT INCHES OF RAINFALL ALONG THE LINE

From the point at Monument No. 1 where the boundary line crawls out of the Rio Grande (at the southeast corner of New Mexico), it strikes west into a wilderness of singularly dry and empty aspect. For 40 miles along this march the traveler must carry his own water.

Near Columbus a few small trees appear, and here, too, a wagon trail from Deming

PRIMITIVE WATER-CARTS IN USE ALONG THE MEXICAN BORDER

In some portions of Mexico the maximum rainfall approaches world records, but in the north, along the border, water rights are at a premium. Feuds, accompanied by the use of dynamite in diverting irrigation channels, have occurred in the cotton-growing lands of Lower California and Sonora. In many cases the supply of water permitted to flow through the irrigation ditches is calculated down to the very minutes per month.

AN ORNATE WROUGHT-IRON GATEWAY TO ONE OF MEXICO'S CITIES OF THE DEAD

Many of the cemeteries of the southern republic suggest the catacombs of Rome and the Campo Santo of Genoa. Tombs are rented by the month or year, and when the relatives of the departed fail to pay the fee required, the sheeted dead are unceremoniously dispossessed, their bones being thrown upon a pile where hundreds of others have suffered a like fate.

down to the American Mormon colonies in Chihuahua crosses the border.

To the west lie the rough, hostile foothills of the Dog Mountains; near here, in the San Luis Range, the line reaches a point 6,600 feet above the sea, marking the continental divide. When that redoubtable outlaw, "The Apache Kid," led his renegade Chiricahuas, they made

this locality their rendezvous; and through this same San Luis Pass runs the old emigrant trail.

Slightly west of the 108th meridian, the line turns at right angles and runs south for a few miles, thence west again.

In the San Bernardino Valley the line strikes the first running water after quitting the Rio Grande—192 miles to the east. Here rises

A SHADY LANE ON A HACIENDA IN SONORA

Small farms are almost unknown in Mexico. The haciendas are vast landed estates embodying many features of the medieval fuedal system. Until a few years ago, the haciendas were in the hands of 6,000 persons among a population of nearly 15,000,000. Some of these estates extended over scores of square miles and had as many as fifty miles of irrigation ditches within their bounds.

the famous Yaqui River, that long, crooked stream that meanders through the vast Mexican State of Sonora and through the turbulent Yaqui Indian zone, finally emptying into the Gulf of California below Guaymas. Thousands of cattle find pasture around the marshy flats of this San Bernardino Valley, and here an old Spanish trading post lies in ruins.

In the whole 700-mile stretch from the Rio Grande to the Pacific, this line crosses only five permanent running streams, and the average rainfall throughout its length is only eight inches.

This border was first fixed by the Treaty of Guadalupe Hidalgo, and subsequently modified by the Gadsden Treaty, or "The Treaty of Mesilla."

In 1891–1896 a new joint commission erected the present monuments, the original heaps of stone having in many places been tampered with or carried away by prospectors for use as mine-boundary markers. These modern tombstone-like obelisks are made of rock where rock is available; in other places cast-iron monuments are set up on cement pedestals. They are never more than five miles apart.

Save the hamlets of Columbus and Hachita, the New Mexican section of this border is almost uninhabited.

WHEN APACHE HUNTING WAS THE GREAT SPORT

Hurdling this line in pursuit of Geronimo and his Apaches was for years a favorite outdoor army sport in these parts; but nowadays most ambitious residents are mining copper, roping and branding cattle, or fussing with irrigation ditches.

Around the camps and corrals, however, many grizzled freighters and post traders of ear-lier days are still loitering; and, true to form, they would rather talk of outlaws, stage-robbers, and historic killings than listen to a farm adviser tell how to outwit weevils or vaccinate a heifer.

One of these old-timers told me how he once slew eight *broncho* Apaches, and then hung them up by their feet to a stout mesquite tree near Lochiel; and that same night a hastening party of Las Cruces peddlers, bound for Hermosillo with a wagon-load of calico, came up and unwittingly camped almost beneath the live oak where the dead Apaches were hanging. Suddenly discovering the terrifying display, the peddlers hastily hitched up and did not make camp till they reached Magdalena, miles to the south.

Today the tamed Apache up around Globe is about the most trustworthy, diligent, and industrious farm laborer to be found in the State; and the two-gun man has gone to the movie studios of California, where the risk is nil and the stakes more certain. Freight wagons along the border are replaced by big auto-trucks, and the old trails are turned into motor highways covered with "camping-out," trippers whose cars bear pennant labels of towns from Peoria to Pasadena.

PUBLIC BATHS WHERE COYOTES RECENTLY ROAMED

Not long ago coyotes were chasing horned toads over an empty desert where Douglas now stands, with libraries, country clubs, theaters, a great Y.M.C.A., public baths, street-cars, and a hotel that might have been lifted bodily out of Cleveland or Kansas City.

The giant smelters at Douglas have run day and night since they were built, a dozen years ago, and have handled thousands of trainloads of ores from Bisbee and Nacozari (in Sonora). At night white-hot streams of molten slag, pouring on the dumps, throw great light

MEXICAN FUEL VENDERS AND PULQUE GATHERERS IN A CACTUS LANE
Thorny cacti such as these provide an almost impenetrable wall, from which even the hardiest trespasser shrinks.

flashes against the sky remindful of Pittsburgh. During a six months' busy period in 1916 the "Copper Queen" and "Calumet and Arizona" smelters handled 131,000,000 pounds of copper, which at, say, 25 cents a pound, would give a value of $32,000,000.

Just over the line from Douglas lies Agua Prieta, from which point an American-owned railway runs south to the mining town of Nacozari, where the model mining camp of all Mexico is operated by the Moctezurna Copper Company, an American corporation.

Drab, dusty Agua Prieta, with its sleepy peons and sad-eyed burros, has a singular faculty of suddenly coming to life and getting front-page publicity from Boston to San Francisco. In its tumultuous recent years it has experienced everything from kidnapping, lynching, and robberies to artillery duels with Villa. Lately a person who coveted his neighbor's mule was found swaying on a rope, with this placard tied to his dangling feet: "He stole mules."

Douglas is about 4,000 feet above sea-level, with 14 inches of rain annually. Ten years ago the land hereabouts was empty. Today artesian wells are flowing—some as much as 600 gallons a minute—caterpillar tractors crawl across the vast Cochise, Sulphur Springs, and Paradise valleys, and the remaining unappropriated land is fast being filed on. There are three methods by which land is secured: direct purchase from the government, homesteading, and under the Desert Land Act.

West of Douglas, eight miles north of Naco, on the line, and quite hidden in the barren Mule Mountains, lies the quaint, up-side-down, busy, hustling Bisbee. Its main street runs up a deep canyon, many of its houses clinging like pigeon cotes to steep hillsides.

In times of freshet, mad torrents tear through it; once water was several feet deep through the lower floors of stores and houses. "Tombstone Street" and "Brewery Gulch" are suggestive of earlier and woollier days.

The popular Borderland Highway, connecting El Paso, Douglas, and Tucson with California, passes this way. Part of this route hereabouts was built with prison labor, under the "honor system" of Governor Hunt.

From Naco, notorious border village astride the line, the El Paso and Southwestern Railway strikes off northwest for Tucson. To the southwest runs a branch of the Southern Pacific of Mexico, serving the great Cananea Consolidated mines (American owned) and connecting at Del Rio, Sonora, with the Nogales branch of the same railway.

West from Naco, conspicuous in the vast grassy stretches of the San Pedro Valley, the straight row of stone monuments marches on, to climb into the wooded Huachuca Range; and a few miles to the northwest lies the shell of ancient, iniquitous, profligate Tombstone.

WHEN TOMBSTONE ACHIEVED FAME

The baffling psychology of names is nowhere more strikingly shown than here. From the day in 1878 when Ed Schiefflin, dodging Apaches, slipped into this canyon with his burros and struck the ledge that made him millions, Tombstone achieved fame. Motor parties on the Overland trail now pass this old prospector's tomb—an odd pyramid of boulders near the spot that made him rich.

Here were such mines as the "Ground Hog" and the "Lucky Cuss." Ore from the latter ran $9,000 a ton. The very name of the town drew the world's attention to it. Here one pioneer jester occasionally issued the famous *Arizona Kicker*, whose heroes used guns that shot

THE HUGE CANDELABRA CACTUS OF MEXICO
OFTEN REACHES A HEIGHT OF SIXTY FEET

The average rainfall along the Mexican border from the Rio Grande to the Pacific is probably less than in any other section of the United States—about eight inches annually, and on the Yuma and Colorado deserts it drops to two or three inches. This boundary line, more than 700 miles in length, crosses only five permanent running streams. It is remarkable that, although arbitrarily chosen, the line from the Rio Grande to the Colorado River follows almost exactly the summit of the divide which separates the waters flowing north into the United States and those flowing south into Mexico.

around corners and up stove-pipes. Another sheet is (or was) named the *Epitaph;* and hereabouts, later on, the lively imagination of Alfred Henry Lewis gave us the "Wolfville" stories.

Climbing the Santa Cruz River west of old Camp Duquesne, the line runs over high, rolling grassy hills scantily covered with stunted live-oaks, and fairly splits in half the important border city of Nogales, entrepôt for all the trade of the Southern Pacific of Mexico. From this point branch lines also strike off north to Tucson and northeast to Benson.

Through this gap in the hills that Nogales now fills runs the ancient trail, worn ages ago by Toltecs and Aztecs and followed later by Spaniards and Jesuits in their advance from Guadalajara to California. Famous Father Keno (or Kuhn, to give him his real name) passed this way, and a few miles north of Nogales, in the Santa Cruz Valley, the ruined mission of Tumacacori (now a national monument) still rears its battered head.

Nearby lies the ancient Presidio of Tubac, where for years a Spanish garrison was kept and whence Don Juan Bautista de Anza set out in 1774 to build a highway to California. It was this same Don Juan who chose the site for San Francisco on the Golden Gate.

Today near Tubac an American rubber company has bought thousands of acres of Santa Cruz Valley land and is farming guayule on a big scale for the manufacture of rubber. Nurseries for propagation of young plants are set up and a model town of cement houses and shady streets for the employees is already built.

Nogales, 3,800 feet above the sea, enjoys a singularly prosperous trade for a town of its size. The declared exports from Mexico run as much as twenty million a year. As at other important border towns, adequate military forces are stationed here, with permanent barracks, hospitals,

recreation halls, and stables. Some 12,000 people live on the American side of the line, and a somewhat lesser number in the Mexican town.

For police purposes, a high barbed wire fence is strung along the boundary line here, dividing the twin cities.

Nogales has foundries, bonded warehouses, strong banks, daily papers, and clubs, and is surrounded by rich mines and profitable cattle ranches.

Nothing along the whole border is more chastely beautiful than the old Mission of San Xavier del Bac, just south of Tucson, on the Nogales highway. It is pure white, visible for miles across the desert, and is built in the form of a cross. It is really one of the great historic memorials of the United States. Nowadays the peaceful Pimas work their little farms and come devoutly to mass in this old church, where years ago other Pimas slew the priests and tried to destroy the building.

A short ride west of Nogales the due-west trend of the line is broken, and it veers northwest by west, straight to the Colorado River, striking that stream a few miles below Yuma.

This part of the boundary was first explored and run by one John Bartlett, after the Treaty of Guadalupe Hidalgo and the Gadsden Purchase. No section of the whole boundary line is so wild, dry, uninhabited, and little known as this which stretches from Sasabe to the Yuma desert. Only a few smugglers, Yaqui gun-runners, and the wary, tireless lineriders who hunt them really know much of this arid, empty waste.

A $600,000 SUBSIDY FOR A STAGE-COACH LINE

After this Gadsden Purchase survey, Congress in 1853 granted money for exploring a railway route from the Mississippi to California; but trains did not run till 31 years later. In 1857, however, mail and passenger stages were started, under a government subsidy of $600,000 a year. This line used 100 Concord stages, 1,000 horses, 500 mules, and about 150 drivers. The fare from St. Louis to San Francisco via this border route was $100. Official orders defined the border route in part as "from Preston, Texas, to the best point of crossing on the Rio Grande, and not far from Fort Fillmore; thence along the new road being opened and constructed, under the direction of the Secretary of the Interior, to Fort Yuma; thence through the best passes and along the best valleys for safe and expeditious staging to San Francisco."

But that part of the trail from Tubac, Arizona, to California was worn and old long before the lumbering Concord stages, making a hundred miles a day, began to use it.

Rafael Amador, an official courier with messages from Santa Ana to the Governor of California, rode from Mexico City to Monterey in some 40 days. Though stripped and robbed by the Yumas and nearly dead of thirst and hunger, he made it.

The coming of General Kearny, with his "Army of the West," to attack the Mexicans in California, in 1847, first mapped out this border trail and made it the main traveled route for the forty-niners. Fully 8,000 passed this way, many dying of thirst. Once in a while prospectors out of Yuma still come upon rusting parts of schooners or whitened bones of men and mules.

Kit Carson, too, made a memorable dash across this desert in '47, with a young army officer named Beale, carrying dispatches from the Fremont party to Washington. (This same Beale later introduced camels into the desert traffic. See footnote, page 34.)

Significant of changing things, scores of well-to-do travelers now desert the comfortable Pullmans to motor along the borderland trails, following the old stage route past historic Tombstone and San Xavier. Most motor tourists, however, use the Santa Fe trail via the Petrified Forest, Flagstaff, and Needles. These motor trails are fairly well maintained and are amply marked with sign-boards as to direction, distances, and the proximity of water and gasoline.

BEEF IS EVERYWHERE

No feature of the trip along this border from El Paso to Nogales is more amazing than the vast numbers of meat-bearing animals to be observed.

Besides introducing the horse, the provident Spaniard also brought cattle, sheep, and goats; and it is probably to Juan de Onate, who reached the Southwest about 1598, that we owe our present wealth of mutton and beef.

As the country was settled, cattle-raising grew as an industry, and, there being no fences, the herder or cowboy was developed. From these Mexican or Spanish *vaqueros* we learned the use of the "rope," or *lariat*—corrupted from *La Riata*. From them, too, we learned to "cut" an animal from a herd, and to brand for identification.

However, due to Indian raids, it was years after Americans entered this region before the cattle industry was safe enough to be profitable.

After Kit Carson rounded up the Navajos at Bosque Redondo, and after Crook gave the Apaches a final walloping at Hell's Hip Pocket (near Fish Creek Hill, on the modern Apache motor road past Roosevelt Dam), the cowman's trade was easier. Then the rise of the cattle

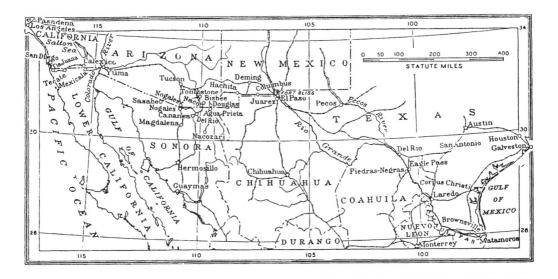

A LONG, CROOKED LINE: THE HISTORIC UNITED STATES-MEXICO BOUNDARY

Some of the wildest and least-known regions of our country are piled up against this border. From the Gulf of Mexico up to El Paso, along the Texas frontier, the Rio Grande forms the boundary; thence to the Pacific coast the line is marked by monuments of stone and iron, so set that one is supposed to be visible from another.

baron began. Might was law, and the sheepman and farmer were out of luck.

Of course, law and order long ago intervened, and the cow and sheep men no longer "draw" on sight and start shooting. But the cowpuncher still has his own opinion of any man who keeps a sheep!

Feuds between rival cow camps are no more; it is no longer good form to brand the other fellow's calves, even if you can "get away with it." Border cattlemen now have associations organized to secure better freight rates, protective laws, and cooperation in marketing cattle. Many cowmen run herds on both sides of the line.

But you can still tell a Texas cowman from his brother in Arizona. The Texas hat, saddle, cinch, bit—even the Texas talk and mental attitude—are quite different from the Arizona article.

At Yuma, where the Southern Pacific now bridges the Colorado, thousands of immigrants were ferried over in days gone by, and Yuma Indians once slew the ferryman and many other whites.

South of Yuma, for a short distance, the Colorado River forms the boundary between the United States and Mexico, the line here running almost north and south. Below the railroad bridge it quits the river, and strikes due west across the Imperial Valley Canal (running into Mexico here), and thence into the sand hills and on to the Imperial Valley.

No other part of the United States is so hot as this. Often the thermometer stands at more than a hundred at midnight; day shade temperatures of 125 Fahrenheit are common. Sahara-like sand-storms blow, so that even stretches of the plank auto road west of Yuma

BENEATH THE INSUFFICIENT SHADE OF A CACTUS BIRD-ROOST

Woodpeckers have dug deep holes for nesting places in this cactus. When the first telegraph lines were run in the southern republic, these birds proved a destructive factor, necessitating the replacement of telegraph poles every year. The cactus in the illustration is one of many varieties which furnish the Mexicans with fruits, sweet-meats, furniture, paper, vinegar, and molasses.

are soon lost in the dunes, and have to be excavated when the storm has passed.

CATTLE SUFFOCATED BY SAND

A tale is told of one poor Arizona cowman who was driving his small herd to the California market. He had just completed the journey across the desert when night overtook his out-fit. With it came a sand-storm. The cattle, lying down thirsty and jaded, were actually covered with the drifting sand, being too tired to stir and keep above it

When dawn came the desert about was covered with mounds and dusty shapes, with here and there a pair of horns protruding. The cattle had suffocated.

Curiously enough, too, steamboats once ran from San Francisco to Arizona! During a period following our Civil War, steamers plied the California coast, came around the peninsula of Lower California into the Gulf, and thence up the Colorado River to Yuma. For many years the main bulk of supplies for the Arizona miners came in this way.

Above Yuma the government's great Laguna Dam proiect is built, and all about the city fertile farms are developed.

Bird life abounds along the Yuma-to-Calexico section of the boundary, especially along the river delta. Here one may see ducks, geese, gulls, brown eagles, hawks, blue herons, *couriers del camino*, or "road-runners," elf owls, hummingbirds, and, among the mountains on the western edge of the Colorado desert, even occasionally that greatest of all American birds, the giant condor. When sitting erect these birds sometimes measure four feet in height.

A prize assortment of reptiles and insects is scattered along this border trail, much discussed by nervous newcomers who "camp out" for the first time.

Rattlers, side-winders, scorpions, centipedes, tarantulas, and the lazy, sluggish Gila monster (*Heloderma suspectum*), to say nothing of the flat, toad-like chuckwalla and a variety of other lizards, live a happy life. Then there are also the banded gekko lizard, the horned toad, and the desert tortoise. (In a lion's den on the Sonora side south of Ajo, I found a number of land tortoise shells, indicating that the lioness had brought these turtles in as food for her young.)

Along the New Mexico and Arizona borders occurs a distinctively interesting bird life. The big Texas "scale quail" has now walked as far west as Sasabe, on the Arizona line. A few years ago it was unknown in these parts.

In his "Distributional List of the Birds of Arizona," Harry S. Swarth gives a total of 362 species and subspecies. Many of these, however, are transients, being winter or summer visitors. In June and July the white-winged Sonora pigeon comes across the border by the tens of thousands. In small, almost dry "tanks," or Arizona ponds, I have shot the crooked bill curlew. Yes, shore-birds in Arizona!

In springtime the desert areas are bright with flowers. New Mexico and Arizona have an indigenous flora almost as large as California. A hundred members of the cactus family are in evidence, affording food to rabbits, gophers, field-rats, birds, beetles, and deer, as well as to cattle and burros. Were it not for their thorns, these plants would probably be utterly destroyed by these troops of hungry animals.

A DESERT LABORATORY ESTABLISHED

To aid farmers in getting better crops, a desert laboratory has been set up near Tucson, where a study of desert plant life is being carried on. Eventually, perhaps, science will help the desert to furnish us with plants good for food and other purposes, even in areas where there is no water for irrigation.

Remnants of the low, filthy Cocopah tribe of Indians still inhabit the mud flats along the delta of the Colorado, catching fish, growing watermelons, or killing rabbits in the *tules* with clubs.

Once I was in the vicinity of Volcano Lake when an aviator had been lost. Other planes came seeking the missing man, roaring and swooping over lagoons and mud flats. Cocopah Indians, loitering near, took only a casual glance at their first aëroplane and went indifferently about their simple tasks.

PACK-ANIMALS LADEN WITH SUPPLIES FOR AMERICAN
TROOPS STATIONED ALONG THE MEXICAN BORDER

The problem of transportation of military supplies along the border is especially difficult owing to the arid character of much of the country, where water as well as food has to be shipped by mule trains. There are still many
stretches of country where the pack-animal is a more practical means of transportation than the motor-truck.

THE YUMA MEDICINE MAN
IS LOSING HIS JOB

If you wander off the beaten trail, say down
below the railroad bridge over the Colorado at
Yuma, you may see a group of naked Yuma Indians sitting in the water up to their necks, their
heads covered with mud to keep cool, "looking
like a herd of seals," as one writer says.

Up near Banning, in the Coahuila settlement, they still have a medicine man, but he is
about out of a job. Sugar-coated pills from the
traders' stores and the free medicine the missionaries pass out appeal more and more.

Their houses are built of poles, arrow-
weed, palm leaves, and willows. Granaries, too,

looking like giant bird nests. are woven from
willows and arrow-weed in dish-like shape.
The basket-weavers, making designs of birds,
turtles, and lizards, are dying out.

A few old tattooed Coahuilas are seen; they
used to employ the mesquite thorn as a needle
and rub the juice of mesquite leaves into the
cuts, thus making a greenish tattoo design.
They eat the chuckwalla lizard; also mesquite
and screwbeans, first pounded fine into flour in
a crude wooden mortar.

By far the most industrious, respectable
Indians in these parts are the Pimas, of southern Arizona. On their reservation southwest of
Tucson these people farm as successfully as the
whites; their work animals are fat; their wagons

are new or freshly painted, and their harness is in repair. With characteristic Indian reserve, they pretend to know no Spanish or English, but under compelling emergency many of them can converse in both languages.

Of our whole border, the California section is best known to Americans because of denser population, excellent motor trails, and proximity of cities like San Diego, Los Angeles, El Centro, and the below-the-sea border town of Calexico, opposite Mexicali. These Imperial Valley twin towns are really one city, split by the international line and each named by peculiar reverse arrangement of the first syllables of the words Mexico and California.

The incredibly fertile Imperial Valley of California sweeps north from Calexico to the Salton Sea, more than 200 feet below sea-level. The oft-told tale of this valley's fight against Colorado River floods and the eventual rise of a thriving community of 60,000 people, with farms worth maybe a hundred million, is one of the romantic stories of this never-say-quit West.

From Calexico the line runs west past Signal Mountain, up the Jacumba Pass over the Lagunas, past the historic border town of Campo (once the stronghold of hellward gentry, now mostly fled, dead, or reformed), through the towns of Tecate and Tia Juana (famous for races and gambling casinos), and thence to the Pacific.

Motor highways parallel the line, one on each side of it, from Calexico-Mexicali to San Diego and Tia Juana. The road on the Mexican side was built by the Mexican Government as a military highway.

The San Diego and Arizona Railway enters Lower California (Mexico) at Tia Juana, rambles east through rocky canyons and cattle-covered, brushy hills for a few miles, and then reënters California at the town of Tecate by tunneling *under* the international line, thus literally forming an underground trail from Mexico into the United States. From here it runs east through Campo, over the mountains and down into the Imperial Valley.

Another road, the International Railway, enters Lower California at Mexicali, winds east some 60 miles or more through a flat, productive cotton country, and then crosses back into California just west of the Colorado River, near Yuma, where it joins the Southern Pacific system.

Such is life along the Mexican border. All kinds of men live here, except poor white men. Few are vastly rich and few are dissatisfied with the country. Immigrants come, conquer the desert, and build comfortable homes. Few ever go back East. Something in the spell of the hazy mountains, the charm of bright skies, and the lure of open ranges holds them here.

And there is no leisure class; everybody *works*. I know one miner worth thirty million. Last summer he sneaked off alone—dodging mail, telegrams, and directors' meetings—to work with his hands for a month, incognito, on the homestead where he'd lived as a boy.

UNCLE SAM'S WORK ON THE BORDER; WHO DOES IT, AND HOW

Uncle Sam's interests along the border are cared for by three branches of the government—the War, Treasury, and Labor Departments—working through the army, the customs, and the immigration services respectively. The State Department is also represented by consuls at the larger Mexican border towns of Matamoras, Laredo, Juarez, Nogales, and Mexicali; but they are concerned only with affairs on Mexican soil.

Since the Diaz régime passed into history, we have kept troops at all *our* border towns, with cavalry patrols between stations. These forces assist local civilian authorities in preserving order and checking the violation of our neutrality laws. They aid in preventing gun-running and the entry into Mexico of expeditions organized in the United States and bent on crossing the line and taking the field against the government of Mexico. About 20,000 of our men, of all arms, are now scattered along the border from Brownsville to San Diego.

The border is divided into three customs districts—the Texas, the New Mexico-Arizona, and the California—and the collectors are stationed at El Paso, Nogales, and Los Angeles. Deputy collectors are stationed at smaller towns, like Brownsville, Laredo, Columbus, Douglas, Naco, Yuma, Calexico, Tecate, etc.

The collectors have wide discretion. Besides the routine duties of their offices, they keep the Treasury Department informed as to economic conditions on the Mexican side of the line.

Then there are the "line riders," a group of mounted customs inspectors. They are a brave, hardy, and resolute class; they know and watch all the cattle trails and smugglers' passes through the remote border sections. Mostly bow-legged, saddle-born, southwesterners, frequently ex-rangers, these solitary men often spend a whole week in the open, sleeping, perhaps, on the ground in bad weather, on a still hunt for the equally capable smuggler.

Frequently enormously valuable cargoes of opium are landed on the Mexican west coast and finally spirited into the United States. A short time ago as much as eighty thousand dollars' worth of "canned hop" is known to have been landed and stored within 60 miles of the line. The profits in this trade are so huge, the tins of opium are so small and easily carried, that the traffic tempts many a crafty man to have a try at quick, easy money. Small-fry smugglers resort to such amateurish expedients as carrying opium over the line in bicycle tires, "trick" suit-cases, or in the tool-boxes of motor cars; but the daring gangs, who "run hop," on a big scale, usually work in armed bands, at night, taking a chance on dodging the line-rider or "shooting it out" with him.

THE MOST DIFFICULT BORDER TASK

Our immigration inspectors have the most difficult task on the border. They must meet, question, and make a record of every alien man, woman, or child that crosses the border. They collect certain head-taxes, and can refuse admission to certain classes (who may appeal).

Many aliens sneak into the country without inspection, crossing the border at lonely, remote points. There are known channels of illicit "underground" traffic. Many Chinese are smuggled in, black porters on trains coming out of Mexico at one time doing a hustling trade. American smugglers have for years engaged in running "yellow contraband" from the Mexican west coast, using speedy motor-boats and landing their hidden passengers as far north as Oakland. As much as $600 a head is sometimes collected on these smuggled immigrants.

BORDER TURMOIL HAS BROUGHT FORTUNES TO MANY

The ill winds that have wasted Mexico have enriched many residents of American border towns. Hundreds of wealthy Mexican families have removed to the border States, depositing their wealth in our banks and business industries.

Banks in certain Yankee border towns have paid as high as 80 percent to 200 percent dividends. Sensational profits have been made on quick cattle deals and fluctuations in Mexican exchange.

Much money was made and lost, too, in the time of the *"billumbiques,"* or fiat money, issued by various factions during the early years of the Mexican revolution. Some of this paper money, originally supposed to be worth two for one (two pesos to one American dollar), finally fell in price until it was quoted at 50 for 1, 100 for 1, and even 1,000 for 1. A tale is told of a poor long-haired Indian at Agua Prieta who went crazy in a barber-shop trying to figure out how many *billumbiques* it would cost him to pay for a hair cut!

Mexican Government purchasing agents come in a constant stream to these frontier towns to buy supplies. They bring suit-cases of money and buy by the carload—buy not only animals, uniforms, provisions, motors, vehicles, harness, guns, ammunition, etc., but they also buy school supplies, machinery, tools, and furniture for use in various government-owned institutions.

In towns like Calexico, El Paso, and Nogales, certain shrewd Americans (mostly born in Poland and Syria), who were mere peddlers or "shoe-string" merchants ten years ago, now own handsome homes, send their children to fashionable schools in the East, and motor out to the California beaches each summer with their wives.

Border brokers make cash advances to speculative traders, who go into Mexico and buy herds of cattle, cargoes of garbanzos and tomatoes, hides and ores. These imports become ready money, once they reach the American side of the line, and the handsome margin of profit stays in the border towns. No part of the United States has seen more prosperity in the last decade than some of these small border ports of entry.

Commission agents, customs brokers, import and export houses, and mining and plantation machinery agents thrive here. The regions of Arizona and New Mexico that crowd against the line are not in themselves particularly rich except in minerals; yet some firms here handle tremendous volumes of goods each year, most of which is sold in Mexico.

Nogales and Douglas have trebled their populations in the past decade, and thousands of Mexicans have moved across the line, increasing the already high percentage of Mexicans residing in our border States.

FROM THE WAR-PATH TO THE PLOW*

By Franklin K. Lane, Secretary of the Interior

ON THE first of last July the Cherokee Indian Nation ceased to exist. This act was the culmination of a treaty promise made over 80 years ago, extended by statute, and at last placed within administrative discretion.

These native and aspiring people have been lifted as American citizens into full fellowship with their civilized conquerors. The Cherokee Nation, with its senate and house, governor and officers, laws, property, and authority, exists no longer.

Surely there is something fine in this slight bit of history. It takes hold upon the imagination and the memory, arouses dreams of the day when the Indian shall be wholly blended into our life, and at the same time draws the mind backward over the stumbling story of our relationship with him.

*An abstract from the annual report to the President of the United States by the Secretary of the Interior.

THE UNITED STATES STILL GUARDIAN

The people of the great Sequoyah have lost their identity, yet—and this is a fact that all do not know—there are still several thousand of these American citizens for whom the United States stands to a greater or less degree *in loco parentis*. We hold our hands upon the property and the private concerns of approximately one-fifth of these "free people."

This seems to be an anomalous situation and prompts at once the inquiry, Has this government a policy with relation to these people and the others of their race? We have had three centuries of contact with the Indian. Do we now know where we are leading him and what our own purpose is with regard to him? Have we aught that may be openly declared as a definite and somewhat immediate aim toward which we can work with clear and unwavering purpose?

If we have such a policy, it should be stated; and this is for love of the Indian himself, who daily asks the question, "What is my future to be at the hands of the white man?"

A BEWILDERED PEOPLE

That the Indian is confused in mind as to his status and very much at sea as to our ultimate purpose toward him is not surprising. For a hundred years he has been spun round like a blindfolded child in a game of blindman's bluff. Treated as an enemy at first, overcome, driven from his lands, negotiated with most formally as an independent nation, given by treaty a distinct boundary which was never to be changed "while water runs and grass grows," he later found himself pushed beyond that boundary line, negotiated with again, and then set down upon a reservation, half captive, half protégé.

What could an Indian, simply thinking and direct of mind, make of all this? To us it might give rise to a deprecatory smile. To him it must have seemed the systematized malevolence of a cynical civilization. And if this perplexed individual sought solace in a bottle of whisky or followed after some daring and visionary Medicine Man who promised a way out of a hopeless maze, can we wonder?

Manifestly the Indian has been confused in his thought because we have been confused in ours. It has been difficult for Uncle Sam to regard the Indian as enemy, national menace, prisoner of war, and babe in arms all at the same time. The United States may be open to the charge of having treated the Indian with injustice, of having broken promises, and sometimes neglected an unfortunate people, but we may plead by way of confession and avoidance that we did not mark for ourselves a clear course, and so, "like bats that fly at noon," we have "spelled out our paths in syllables of pain."

THE INDIAN'S STATUS

There are some 300,000 Indians in the United States. This grand total includes all who are of Indian blood or who have been adopted into the tribes. The census figure of 1910 shows an Indian population of 304,950, as contrasted, it may be noted, with a population in 1860 of 254,300.

These are for the most part wards in chancery, the government being the chancellor. They live in large part on reservations, which are little more than expanded and perhaps somewhat idealized orphan asylums. They have lands aggregating in extent 109,150 square miles, or a territory equal to that of Maine, New Hampshire, Vermont, Massachusetts, Rhode Island, Kentucky, and Virginia, and worth, by rough estimate, six hundred million dollars.

THE WEALTHIEST PEOPLE IN THE WORLD

Over two-thirds of this land is now held as individual farms, the unallotted or tribal lands being estimated as worth less than $200,000,000. If an appraisement were made of the full value of the timberlands and of the oil and coal lands, and added to this was the value of the herds and personal property of the Indians, it is probable that they would be found to have a wealth approximating $900,000,000. In moneys, the Treasury of the United States has trust or tribal funds approximating $50,0000,000, while in the banks throughout the country we have deposited to the credit of individual Indians under our control something over $18,000,000.*

---

*The general allotment act of 1887 was the first step toward the setting aside for each Indian of a tract of land

FIVE HUNDRED CATTLE READY FOR ISSUE TO INDIANS: STANDING ROCK

The valuable grazing lands of the Indians offer unusual opportunities for increasing the meat supply of the country. They have what are regarded as the most desirable grazing lands in unbroken bodies in the United States. Last year about $1,500,000 was expended in buying horses, cattle, and sheep to stock these lands and to establish large tribal stock ranches. Heretofore Indian grazing lands have been rented to white ranchmen.

which he could develop by his own efforts and on which he could construct a home for himself and for his family.

Each of the 41,698 members of the Cherokee Tribe receive an allotment of 110 acres of the average allottable lands, valued originally at $325.60. The average Cherokee family may be said to number four persons, which would give to it 440 acres of land. The Choctaws and Chickasaws, the Creeks and the Seminoles have also received allotments and their tribal funds are being divided.

The Osages are probably the wealthiest people in the world. The average wealth of the Osage Indian is $9,579.85, and 2,230 Osages each received approximately 657 acres of land as allotments. The average income of the Osages from oil and gas royalties is $690.89. For an average family of four this would make an annual income of approximately $2,700, to say nothing of the large income from the lands allotted to them. Some few families have an income of $12,000 per year.

The individual wealth of the Indian necessarily depends upon the value of his individual allotment; as, for instance, in the Creek Nation, one of the Five Civilized Tribes, the great oil fields have brought wealth to those Indians so fortunate as to hold allotments within the oil territory. The following cases are examples of the royalties for 1914 received by Indians of the Creek Nation from oil: Samuel Richard, $94,000: Jeannetta Richard, $90,000; Seeley Alexander, $57,000; Lessey Yarhola, $73,000; Eastman Richard, $93,000; Thomas Long, $35,000; Ella Jones, $31,000; Nancy Yarhola, $29,000; Johnston Wacoche, $27,000; Miller Tiger, $23,000.

Some of the Bad River Indians have received as high as from $14,000 to $16,000 for the timber cut from their allotments.

On the other hand, we must not forget that many of the Indians have lands which are little better than sand hills, that even though these tribes have vast herds of sheep and the wealth of the tribe seems large, when divided pro rata shares it would be but a small sum which could quickly be expended for subsistence.

WOLF EAGLE AND RELATIVES: BLACKFEET TRIBE

The Indians of the United States own lands almost equalling in area those of all New England and New York. A rough estimate places the value of these lands at $600,000,000. If to this be added their holdings of timber, etc., they would probably be found to be worth not far from a billion dollars.

MUST THE INDIAN REMAIN A WARD OF THE GOVERNMENT FOREVER?

The function which this government is performing for these Indians is to care for their personal welfare, supervise their business affairs, improve their property, hold their moneys, give education to their children, care for their sick, protect them from their enemies, and insure them against starvation.

This surely is doing much for a people who are richer on the average than the majority of our own people. And, we ask, must this governmental activity persist? Must this burden

TYPICAL HOME OF FLATHEAD INDIANS
ON THE FLATHEAD RESERVATION: MONTANA

"The Osages are probably the wealthiest people in the world. The average wealth of the Osage Indian is $9,570.85, and 2,230 Osages each received approximately 657 acres of land as allotments. The average income of the Osages from oil and gas royalties is $690.89. For an average family of four this would make an annual income of approximately $2,700, to say nothing of the large income from the lands allotted to them. Some few families have an income of $12,000 per year" (see text, page 54).

always rest upon the people of this country? Is it for the benefit of the Indian himself that it should continue?

There are those who say that it should not last a single day. The American conscience, however, our sense of justice, our traditions, in fact, will not permit the adoption of a drastic course that would cast the Indian upon a world for which he is ill-prepared.

Yet I am of the opinion that it would be better, far better, to sever all ties between the Indian and the government, give every man his own and let him go his own way to success or destruction, rather than keep alive in the Indian the belief that he is to remain a ward of the government. The advocates of the sink or swim policy may be reckless. The advocates of the almshouse policy are surely doing harm.

Is there, then, no way out? Must we go blunderingly on without goal and without policy?

KILLING "THE
ORPHAN ASYLUM" IDEA

The way out is gradually and wisely to put the Indian out. Our goal is the free Indian. The orphan-asylum idea must be killed in the mind of Indian and white man. The Indian should

BLACKFEET INDIAN AND FAMILY: MONTANA

"The political conditions of the world will make the next few years a period of great prosperity for the American farmer. Let us see that the Indian, with his broad acres, is in truth an American farmer, and that he properly participates in this unusual opportunity."

know that he is upon the road to enjoy or suffer full capacity. He is to have his opportunity as a "forward-looking man."

This is not my dictum, for the government has been feeling its way toward this policy for nearly 40 years. This is the rationale of the whole of our later congressional policy, of the liberality of Congress toward the education of the Indian, of the allotment system, of limitations fixed upon disposition of property.

If the course of Congress means aught it means that the Indian shall not become a fixture as a ward.

It is the judgment of those who know the Indian best, and it is my conclusion, after as intimate a study as practicable of his nature and needs, that we should henceforth make a positive and systematic effort to cast the full burden of independence and responsibility upon an increasing number of the Indians of all tribes.

APACHE PAPOOSE AND BASKETS: ARIZONA

"There are some 300,000 Indians in the United States. This grand total includes all who are of Indian blood or who have been adopted into the tribes. The census figure of 1910 shows an Indian population of 304,950, as contrasted, it may be noted, with a population in 1860 of 254,300', (see text, page 53).

BLACKFEET INDIANS AT WORK ON THEIR IRRIGATION PROJECT

"The great oil fields have brought wealth to those Indians so fortunate as to hold allotments within the oil territory. The following cases are examples of the royalties for 1914 received by Indians of the Creek Nation from oil: Samuel Richard, $94,000, Jeannetta Richard, $90,000; Seeley Alexander $57,000; Lessey Yarhola, $73,000; Eastman Richard, $93,000; Thomas Long, $35,000; Ella Jones, $31,000; Nancy Yarhola, $29,000; Johnston Wacoche, $27,000; Miller Tiger, $23,000. Some of the Bad River Indians have received as high as from $14,000 to $16,000 for the timber cut from their allotments" (see text, page 54).

The irrigable lands belonging to the Indians form one of the principal sources of wealth of these people, and also form probably the best opportunity for these people to become individually self-supporting. In some sections of the country the Indians are better acquainted with irrigation farming than the whites in the same communities, and they are making great success in this line.

I find that there is a statute which significantly empowers the Secretary of the Interior to do this in individual cases. That authority is adequate. And as soon as the machinery of administration can be set in motion I intend to use such authority. If year by year a few from each of the tribes can be made to stand altogether upon their own feet, we will be adding to the dignity of the Indian race and to their value as citizens. To be master of himself, to be given his chance—this is the Indian's right when he has proven himself. And all that we should do is to help him to make ready for that day of self-ownership.

PREPARING THE INDIAN TO STAND ALONE

Viewed in this light, the Indian problem is incomparably larger today than it was when the Cherokees were gathered up from the Southern States and sent into the unknown across the Mississippi. In 1830 the problem was how to get the Indians out of the way. Today the problem is how to make him really a part of the nation.

This blend of wisdom, dignity, and childishness, this creature of a non-commercial age, has been brought into a new day when all must live by conforming to a system that is as foreign to him as the life of the Buddhistic ascetic would be to us. Slowly through a century and more of torturous experience he has come to see that it is not our purpose to do him harm; but he must learn to find his place in an economy that antagonizes every tradition of his ten thousand years of history.

How, then, are we to get into the mind of this soldier-sportsman the fact that the old order has passed away, and that the gentleman of today earns his right to live by his usefulness; that the American cannot be a man and a ward at the same time?

It is a strange thing indeed that we should be concerning ourselves so largely and spending so many millions each year for the remaking of the people who are the truest of Americans. It shows how anxious to be just and willing to be generous are our people. They feel with a quick conscience how cruel it would be to introduce this primitive man into a harsh, competitive world of business with a code of its own more foreign to him than that of the Bushido; too much, they fear, like pitting Little Boy Blue against Shylock in a trade.

Let us frankly state the fact—there is such a thing as being too unselfish, and this the Indian too often is, for he has not gained a forecasting imagination. His training has not given him the cardinal principle of a competitive civilization, the self-protecting sense. It is not instinctive in him to be afraid of starving tomorrow if he is generous or wasteful today.

"WHY SHOULD WE WORK?"

And work? Why work if not necessary? Is it not, as an Osage chief once reprovingly said to me, is it not the hope of every American that he may some day be a gentleman who does not work?

We are bent, then, upon saving the Indian from those who would despoil him until the time comes when he can stand alone. And that time comes when he has absorbed into his nature the spirit of this new civilization of which he has become a part. This is certainly a revolution we are expecting—an impossible revolution in some natures—the substitution of a new standpoint for one long taught by fathers and grandfathers.

Truly such a transformation is not to be worked like some feat of legerdemain, by a turn of the wrist. Bayonets cannot do it; money cannot do it. We can force men to work. We can keep them without work. These two methods we have tried with the Indian, and they have failed in leading him toward the goal of responsible self-support. Adaptation to new environment comes from education through experience.

We therefore have the task of introducing a new conception into the Indian mind. This is not a thing that can be done wholesale. It becomes an individual problem, and our hope lies in schools for the young and in casting more and more responsibility upon the mature and letting them accept the result.

What should the test be in passing upon the fitness of one who is to be sent out into the world? Plainly his ability to handle himself, to care for himself so that he will not become a charge on the community. To be a rich Indian is not a qualification, for his wealth may indicate, and generally does, nothing more than good fortune. In the land lottery some drew prizes and some blanks. Nor should the degree of blood be the test nor education; for many of those who are wisest in counsel and most steady in habits and sturdy in character are uneducated full-bloods. The man who can "do" for himself is the man to be released. And he is the man who thinks not in terms of the Indians' yesterday, but in terms of the Indians' tomorrow. One whose imagination can take that leap and whose activities will not lag behind. It is to be remembered that we are not looking for an ideal Indian nor a model citizen, but for one who should not longer lean upon the government to manage his affairs.

MANY THOUSANDS
ARE CAPABLE AND THRIFTY

There are many thousand Indians in our charge who are entirely self-supporting, capable, thrifty, far-sighted, sensible men; and, singularly enough, these are most often found among those tribes which were most savage and ruthless in making war upon the whites. Some of these are indeed so far-sighted that they do not wish to enjoy full independence because their property would then become subject to taxation.

Others are attached by a tribal sentiment and by the natural conservatism of the Indian to existing conditions. Still others are held to governmental control in part because of the entanglement of their tribal affairs. The government will not do its duty toward itself or toward these Indians until men of this class are fully released. There is a second class, made up of those willing to work but not knowing how, and a third class, of those who know but have no tools. For these there is help—the teacher farmer for the one and a small loan in the form of tools for the other.*

*EXTRACTS FROM LETTERS FROM INDIANS

"You can't make the Indian independent by doing his business for him."—*A Kickapoo Indian.*

"Indians ought to live like men—not like boys."—*A Colorado Ute.*

"We will never better our condition while we are wards of the nation."—*A Yakima Indian.*

"As long as we have money in the U. S. Treasury we will not do much work, and work is our salvation."—*An Oklahoma Kiowa*

"Government should not listen to the plea of a few backward Indians who are opposed to progress and are contented to live at the expense of government and of industrious Indians."—*An Iowa Sac and Fox.*

"My children attend public schools; I pay taxes; why should I be under government supervision?"—*An Oregon Indian.*

"The government cannot all the time take care of the Indians."—*A Wisconsin Indian.*

"Indians now hampered by delays, regulations, and red tape . . . and these things have made them discouraged."—*A Tulalip Indian.*

"No greater blessing could come to the Indian than to be compelled to think for himself."—*An Oklahoma Seminole.*

THE APACHE AND THE CACTUS: ARIZONA'S PIONEERS

For centuries the Indians of the Papago country, in southern Arizona, lived in a semi-arid region, eking out a scant existence from lands covered with cacti and sage-brush. It has been discovered that under those lands lies a rich supply of water in an underground stratum, which brought to the surface and used for irrigation, will make their country flow with milk and honey. It it the intention of the government to sink wells and use this water for the benefit of the ten thousand or more Indians who live in that region.

There are those, too, for whom it is too great a jump to pass from hunting to farming, but who can herd cattle, and for these the government is providing herds for their ranges. Congress has been liberal in its appropriations for these things, and with a stable policy and administrative efficiency these Indians can be gradually lifted into usefulness, full self-support, and into entire independence.

THE ORATOR AND THE LOAFER

Then there is the "proud" red man who idly clings to the traditions of his race and talks of its past with such dignified eloquence, declaring in one glowing moment against the injustice of requiring service from those who once owned the continent and in the next sentence pleading for rations. This man is half brother to him who has degenerated under the orphan-asylum system into a loafer. My confidence is that for all these there is some hope, for most of them much.

But from what has been already said it will be perceived that in the direction of Indian affairs I believe it wisest to give our chief concern to those who are willing to work, who show evidence of a rudimentary ambition, and to convert the Bureau of Indian Affairs into a great coöperative educational institution for young and old, reducing to the minimum the eleemosynary side of its work and its trust functions. It sounds trite, but it has its significance here, that it is not so important to conserve the wealth of a people as to develop their capacity for independence.

For the young the schools* are doing much, especially the day schools on the reser-

vations. By way of answer to those who are troubled at the neglect of the Indian, it may be noted that since 1863 we have expended $85,000,000 in the education of the Indian. Beginning with $20,000 a year, the annual appropriation for this purpose now reaches nearly $4,500,000. Those schools are most useful in which emphasis is laid upon the industrial side of life. There are no better schools, I am well advised, than many of our reservation schools, where each child is taught the rudiments of learning and to be useful in practical things—reading, writing, and arithmetic; how to plow and sow, hoe and harvest; how to build a house and shoe a horse, or cook a meal, make a dress, and nurse a sick man or animal.

SOWING SEEDS OF AMBITION

In one thing we are short—the art of inducing ambition. This largely depends upon the genius of the teacher to fire the imagination of the pupil, for, after all, the true teacher is an inspirer, and the only thing he teaches his people

---

*It is reported that there are 84,229 Indian children of school age. Of these 6,428 are ineligible for school, leaving 77,801 eligible for school. Of this number 22,775 children are in government schools, as follows: In the 37 nonreservation boarding schools conducted outside of the Indian country there are enrolled 10,857 children. In the reservation boarding schools situated on the various reservations there are 9,700, and in the government day schools on the reservations, which resemble closely the ordinary district schools of the States, except that they offer industrial training, there are 7,218 children. Of the children enrolled in mission schools there are 1,379 in mission boarding schools under contract with the government and 3,450 in mission schools without contract. There are enrolled in the public and private schools 25,924 Indian pupils of which the Indian Office has record. This would leave 15,906 Indian children eligible for school privileges, but not reported as being in school. Of this number probably 6,000 in the Navajo and Papago country are without school facilities, but the greater part of the remainder are enrolled undoubtedly in public schools, but not reported.

A SHEEP CORRAL: HOPI LAND ORAIBI, ARIZONA

"To teach the Indian that he must work his way, that the government will no longer play the part of Elijah's raven, to convert the young to our civilization through the creation of ambitions and desires which the blanket life cannot satisfy; to organize each group of Indians into a community of sanely guided coöperators, who shall be told and taught that this government is not to continue as an indulgent father, but as a helpful, experienced, and solicitous elder brother—this program we are adventuring upon" (see text, page 65).

is to want something. That is the first step in all civilization.

We need teachers in the Indian Service, men and women with enthusiasm and with sympathy, not learned, but wise. We are to control less and to help more. Paternalism is to give way to fraternalism. The teachers we need are helpers, farmers, and nurses, who may not know how to write ideal reports, but do know how to trust and secure trust. There is no way by which an Indian can be made to do anything, but experience justifies the belief that there are many ways by which he can be led.

To turn the Indian loose from the bonds of governmental control, not in great masses, but individually, basing this action upon his ability to watch his steps and make his way, not in any fool's dream that he will advance without tripping, but in the reasonable hope that he will develop self-confidence as he goes along; to destroy utterly the orphan-asylum idea, giving charity only to the helpless and in gravest emergencies; to teach the Indian that he must work his way, that the government will no longer play the part of Elijah's raven; to convert the young to our civilization through the creation of ambitions and desires which the blanket life cannot satisfy; to organize each group of Indians into a community of sanely guided coöperators, who shall be told and taught that this government is not to continue as an indulgent father, but as a helpful, experienced, and solicitous elder brother—this program we are adventuring upon. It may be inadequate, but it is surely a long step on the road which the Cherokees took.

PROTECTING THE INDIAN FROM HIS ENEMIES

To carry out this policy there should be continuity of purpose within Congress and within the Department of the Interior. The strength of the Administration should be turned against the two enemies of the Indian—those who, out of sentiment or for financial reasons, keep the Indian's mind turned backward upon the alleged glories of other days and the injustices that have been done him, and those who would unjustly take from him the heritage that is his.

The demands now being urged that reservations shall be broken up to make way for white men who can use the lands to better advantage should be resisted, unless it can be shown that the Indians under proper stimulus will not use these lands, or that by the sale of a portion the Indians would be enabled to make greater use of the remainder. The Indian is no more entitled to idle land than a white man.

But speculation is not use; and the Indian must be regarded as having the first call upon the lands now his, at least until white men are willing to surrender their lands when not used. Idle Indians upon idle lands, however, must lead to the sale of the lands, for the pressing populations of the West will not long look upon resources unused without strenuous and effective protest, and the friend of the Indian who would give him his chance and would save for him his property is he who keeps in mind the thought of his future instead of his past, and that future depends upon his willingness to work.

LITTLE-KNOWN PARTS OF PANAMA

By Henry Pittier

Author of "Costa Rica—Vulcan's Smithy"
in the National Geographic Magazine

THE usual tourist, fresh from a visit to the gigantic work now nearing completion between the cities of Colon and Panama, will tell of his occasional glimpses of the virgin forest and of his experiences with the natives, supplementing his narrative perhaps with pictures of the jungle and of what he took for aboriginal Indians.

In fact if our friend has followed the customary route, limiting his itinerary to a train ride from Colon across to Panama, with stops at Gatun and Pedro Miguel, to inspect the locks, and at Culebra to see the big cut, he knows very little of the real country, and in ninety-nine cases out of a hundred his native Indians are likely to have had African features.

There is, undeniably, plenty of jungle and thicket along the future canal, but it is almost wholly second growth; and in those places where the primeval vegetation has been spared, as in the swampy lowlands between Gatun and Bohio and on the steeper declivities of the hills, it is and has always been more or less stunted

and scarce and so does not give an adequate idea of the majestic forests that still cover about two-thirds of the territory of the Republic of Panama.

If, however, our tourist is a man of leisurely habits, a stranger to the hurried ways of the present generation, he may leave the beaten track, pick up the wanderer's stock, and go tramping over the excellent roads built parallel to the railroad and the canal by the government of the Canal Zone. He will then meet occasionally some last vestiges of the aboriginal vegetation and examples of the wonderful rankness of tropical plant life.

Not far from Pedro Miguel, on the way to Panama, stands a cluster of Cavanillesia trees, once part of the forest, but today shading a pasture (see picture, page 70). Apart from the striking effect of their huge straight trunks, which are out of proportion with their insignificant flat crowns, these particular specimens are of especial interest on account of the fact that they grow nearly at the extreme northwestern

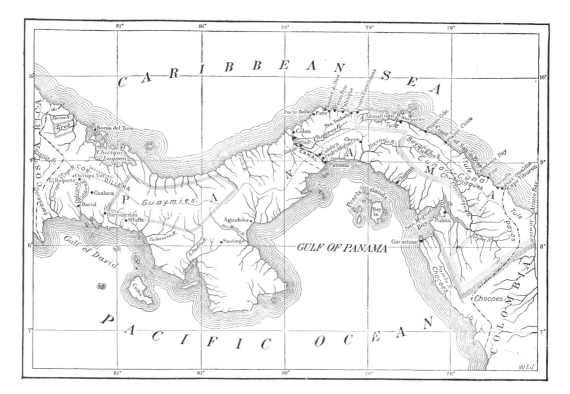

SKETCH MAP OF PANAMA, SHOWING GENERAL FEATURES
AND PRESENT LOCATION OF ABORIGINAL TRIBES

areal limit of the species. Eastward, in Colombia, it seems to reach the Magdalena River, and southward it can be followed along the coastal plains as far as Peru.

It may be interesting to add that the fruit affords a good example of the wonderful contrivances by means of which nature insures the propagation of the species. The fruit is an elongate spindle, provided with five broad wings and very light, so that it travels easily far away from the parent tree. The small seeds are imbedded in the woody tissue of the spindle, and the surrounding cells are filled with a gum which readily absorbs available moisture and swells to a considerable extent. When the fruit reaches the ground, the seeds thus find themselves at once immersed in an overflowing, gelatinous mass of gum, which furnishes the water necessary to the first stages of germination.

Another vegetable wonder that grows among the bushes on sandy flats along streams is often detected by the delightful odor and the yellow bright color of its singular fruits. It is the candle-tree, now introduced into most botanical gardens of the tropics, but a native of the central part of Panama.* The beautiful *Gustavia superba* should also be mentioned as a special feature of the Isthmian flora.

*See NATIONAL GEOGRAPHIC MAGAZINE, vol. xxiii, p. 124, 1912.

In thus wandering across country, instead of keeping exclusively to railroad trains, the traveler will have occasion many times to wonder at the incredible luxuriance of vegetable life in general and to observe the never-ending struggle for supremacy.

As to the real Indians, he may succeed in getting a look at some male specimen along the wharves at Colon or around the market in Panama City; but the chances are that they will mostly pass unnoticed in the motley crowd of mixed races of the larger towns. At least eight-tenths of the native inhabitants of the Republic show to a more or less marked extent the stamp of African blood, and the most extraordinary cases of interbreeding are observed everywhere.

East of the canal, however, and not taking the aboriginal tribes into consideration, the negro element vastly predominates, the settlements of Porto Bello, Nombre de Dios, Palenque, and Viento Frio, on the Caribbean Sea, being formed, as it seems, by descendants of both West Indians and Spanish slaves, and the villages of the Pacific coast—Chepo, Chiman, Garachine—and those in the Tuyra basin by the latter only. West of the canal the predominance of the African element becomes less marked, at least on the southern side of the country, as one goes farther toward Chiriqui, where whites and Indians are more predominant.

Panama is hardly a country for mountaineering, most of its area being below the 3,000-foot contour line. The highest elevations are in the western part, which is an extension of the Costa Rican system. There the Chiriqui Peak, or Volcan de Chiriqui, as it is more commonly called, attains 11,000 feet and is worth ascending. Farther eastward and on the main divide several bold peaks can be seen from both coasts; they very likely reach the 10,000-foot

line, but they have never been ascended and their exact altitudes, names, and even their true geographic position are still to be recorded.

The same can be said of the eastern-most group of high ranges, on the Colombian border, an undeciphered mass of domes and peaks, which have never been explored and whose real relation to the western Cordillera of Colombia has never been ascertained. It is almost certain, however, that they form an independent system, and that the old notion of the South American Andes forming also the backbone of the Central American Isthmus should no longer appear as it often does, in modern writings.

From the naturalist's standpoint these highest mountains at both ends of the Panamanian territory are of special interest. As few or no collectors have ever visited them, they are likely to be the abode of many unknown forms of both vegetable and animal life. They are also the most advanced outposts of the fauna and flora of the neighboring countries. Besides, they are attractive even to the ordinary tourist, on account of their beautiful scenery and of the marvelous changes observed within a few hours as one rises from the lower to the upper regions, experiencing at the same time a corresponding variation in climatic conditions. This is best seen in the ascent of the Chiriqui Volcano, the summit of which can be reached in three days from David, by way of El Boquete.

ASCENDING THE CHIRIQUI VOLCANO

David stands at about 12 miles from the seashore, in an open, slightly undulating country. It is one of the most rapidly improving towns of Panama, on account of the varied and abundant resources offered by the surrounding country and the affluence of foreign, mostly American, settlers. The tidal belt ends in the neighboring bottoms, and the plain between the sea and the first hills is subdivided into two or three terraces, the highest of which is about 150 feet above sea-level.

The deep ravines, cut through these terraces by the many streams descending from the mountains, allow an insight into the recent geological history of the district. Thick layers of a fine sand, almost horizontal and apparently devoid of organic remains, show that the whole plain is an ancient sea-bottom, uplifted at a not very remote time either by some sudden cataclysm, or insensibly by the slow process that governs the emergence and subsidence of coastal lands all over the globe.

In former explorations, in the adjoining part of Costa Rica, I have noticed the same indications of a general upheaval, the neck of the Osa Peninsula still showing unmistakable evidences of a recent broad sea-channel, and bluffs, bearing the peculiar relief due to the action of the waves, lifted to nearly 300 feet above sea-level.

Most of the flat country about David is utilized as grazing land, and during the dry season it is constantly swept by the strong trade wind, reaching over the mountains through the deepest depressions of the Cordillera. Only in sheltered places along the rivers, behind the knolls that rise here and there, and around the houses, is there any show of arboreous vegetation, among the most conspicuous representatives of which may be cited the algarrobo and the corotú. The tamarind and mango, two East Indian trees now naturalized all over the tropics, and the native wine and plum palms, are the trees most generally seen around the houses. Extensive forests, displaying the luxuriance and generous proportions of real tropical vegetation, are found only at some distance to the west, on

the lands adjoining the Chiriqui Viejo River, or to the east between Gualaca and Horconcitos.

Going north in the direction of the Chiriqui Peak, one is soon struck by the peculiar range of low hills running, as it seems, between the plains and the mountains and parallel to the sea-coast. The road winds between these and, mostly following the Dolega River, ascends gradually toward E1 Boquete. The general incline is so insensible that one travels nearly 25 miles before reaching the foot of the volcano, at an altitude of about 3,000 feet. The ride is mainly across savannas or through what ecologists call a parklike landscape.

During the dry season the long stretches, bare of arboreous vegetation, are constantly swept by the north trade wind which attains its major intensity between 9 o'clock a. m. and 3 o'clock p. m., and is often of such violence that even the horses find it difficult to stand and to proceed on their way. Every detail of the surrounding landscape bears the impress of the wind. In the most exposed places the surface of the soil is submitted to an active aerial erosion, the minute particles of the ground being whisked away the moment they become loose.

The meager sod is characteristic in appearance, consisting not of a continuous carpet of grasses, as in most savannas, but of isolated tufts of sedges and small plants (mainly Leguminosae and Rubiaceae), distinguished by the unusual development of their root system.

Many an acre is absolutely bare, and at places long stretches of stones, running from north to south, are explained by the natives as being remnants of former eruptions of the volcano. They are really what is left of low ridges demolished by the wind.

In hollow places, as along the dry bed of creeks that flow only during the wet season, the trees show some attempts at congregating in

CAVANILLESIA LANDSCAPE NEAR PEDRO MIGUEL: CANAL ZONE

Besides their interest as a remnant of the primeval forest, these trees grow nearly at the extreme northwestern areal limit of the species, which is mainly a feature of the South American Pacific coast (see page 66).

small groves; but they have a stunted appearance, their trunks are twisted and knotty, their limbs few, and all strikingly growing in a southerly direction (see page 74).

The few head of cattle browsing through these thinned savannas are shaggy, and even the people and their dwellings, the former with their large hats tied upon the head and the latter with roofs half gone or mended temporarily with the leaves of the native royal palm, show the permanent action of the wind.

Not to impress the reader too deeply with the dreary barrenness of the country, it should be added that the southside exposures of the hills and the deeper valleys offer sheltered nooks, with prosperous villages surrounded by patches of grassy pastures and of forests.

Through this rather desolate region several rivers have cut deep, narrow canyons, in which subtropical vegetation is mixed in a curious way. Oaks are seen growing next to palms, giant elms mingling their branches with those of towering ficus, and, among herbaceous plants, clematis and nettles side by side with showy bignonias and fragrant epiphytic orchids. Bathed in the perpetual but never excessive dampness of the foaming river, sheltered from wind and strong nightly radiation by the high surrounding walls, and with an atmosphere incessantly renewed, the hidden recesses of these gorges assume, indeed, a singularly beautiful appearance. They are, however, difficult of access, and not only teem with insect life, but offer favorite refuge for snakes, which are attracted by the latter and by the many small mammals.

Near El Boquete the road leaves the savannas to penetrate into the upper Caldera Valley. This is the favorite summer resort of the Panamanians and of many Canal Zone Americans, and also the only coffee-growing section of the whole Republic. On account of the prohibitive tariff, the latter is one of the best paying products of native agriculture, and several foreigners have established here prosperous plantations. But El Boquete, half in the windy, semi-arid zone and half in that of continued rains, has a very limited producing capacity, and cannot by far supply the rapidly increasing coffee consumption of the larger centers. It is not equipped, either, for a summer resort, as the "Hotel de Lino" is simply a farmhouse, where abundant meals and a kindly hospitality are the welcome but sometimes inadequate compensations for the lack of worldly comfort.

To the lover of nature, however, the surrounding forests are forever a source of healthy enjoyment, among which orchid hunting is not the least exciting. Several of the most highly prized species hide on the moss-grown trees, and often their exquisite perfume is the only indication of their near presence. Now and then the eye is attracted by white or pink patches of Trichopilias, or by the curiously shaped although less conspicuous flowers of some Catasetum (page 80).

The visit to the Chiriqui Volcano is usually made from here. It is an 8,000-foot ascent to the top. Not that it offers any danger or even chances of dramatic situations, but it is a straight and exhausting climb, rendered difficult at times by the unsteadiness of the loose soil, the intricate thickets, and, even in the upper belt, by high, tangled grassfields. Rocks,

all of volcanic origin, are seen only in deep gorges or near the top; snow and ice are out of the question; and, though still called a volcano, the Chiriqui Peak is a dead one, in which only obsolete traces of former plutonic action are to be seen.

Still, the ascent is worthwhile, if made at the right time. The trail leads first through savannas and beautiful oak forests, mixed with sweet cedars and other subtropical trees, and as it goes higher and higher, always straight toward the top without any superfluous windings, the attention of the traveler is distracted from his toilsome physical exertion by the successive appearance, in the middle of a strange vegetation, of many familiar-looking plants, like trailing bramble vines loaded with luscious blackberries, less welcome nettles, just like those seen around old farm-houses in northern climates, alders, and the like. A formal investigation of the flora of the upper mountain belt would show, in fact, that it is a mixture of a reduced endemic element with representatives of the flora of our northern countries and of the South American Andes.

It may be interesting to mention here that along the trail, between two and three thousand meters of elevation, there are whole forests of a Persea tree, which is a very near relative to the alligator pear. It grows below and above the frost-line, and we have repeatedly advised its acclimatization in California where it could perhaps be used as a grafting or budding stock. On account of its hardiness, it is not unlikely that by its means the extreme limit of alligator-pear cultivation could be shifted a good distance northward.

The long ascent to the top is not made in one day. There is a first camp in a picturesque gorge, about half way up from El Boquete, and then another at the bottom of the large northern crater, in one of the nooks formed by the narrow gorges leading to the highest summit. Here the temperature goes every night near or below the freezing point, and the cold is very intense to people accustomed to the heat of the lower plains.

But during the dry season the air is so crisp and pure, the sky so blue, the song of the thrushes and of many other familiar little birds so pathetically lovely, and the beautiful surrounding nature so exhilarating, that one easily forgets small bodily inconveniences to enjoy with full heart the beauty of it all.

The crater is a circular plain about 2,000 feet in diameter, surrounded by a more or less broken ridge that is densely covered with a forest of myrtles, oaks, and less familiar trees. The culminating peak is distant only about two hours' climb, and as one approaches it the arboreal vegetation becomes more and more stunted and dwarfed, until it completely disappears, to give place to rocks and grassy slopes.

In clear weather the panorama from the summit is splendid: to the south, the vast expanse of the Pacific and the beautiful lowlands of Chiriqui, all interlaced forests and savannas; to the north, a labyrinth of unexplored valleys, covered totally by virgin forest running down to the Caribbean Sea; westward, the Costa Rican mountains familiar to the writer; and to the east, many a lofty peak of no despicable prominence and virgin yet of any tourist's footprints. In our ascent we had only glimpses of all this, as a thick fog was gathering at the time. From the top we had only a momentary vision of a far-looking silvery ribbon, the Rio Chiriqui Viejo, several thousand feet below us to the west.

The return trip can be effected easily in one day.

THE ABORIGINAL TRIBES OF PANAMA

Our tramp through Panama now takes us to scenes quite different from those we have just described, among what is left of the aborigines of the country.

In the years 1501 to 1503, when Rodrigo de Bastidas and Christopher Columbus visited the northern coast of the Isthmus, they found it densely populated. About ten years later Balboa met with identical conditions along the southern coast, and all subsequent reports of early explorers give evidences of the fact that the whole country was in possession of numerous clans, the names of many of which have been preserved.

The two principal nations were the Guaymies, extending from the Chiriqui Volcano eastward to what is today the Canal Zone, and the Cuna-Cuna, on the opposite side of the Isthmus. West of the volcano, in the valleys of the Chiriqui Viejo, Changuena and Diquis rivers, and possibly a little farther east, along the Pacific Ocean, were the Dorasques, a warlike and more civilized race, to whom the beautiful pottery and the gold ornaments found in the ancient graves of Chiriqui are often attributed. As can be deduced from these relics, the Dorasques had trade relations with the Niquirans and Chorotegans, of Costa Rica, and through them felt in some degree the influence of the Nahuatl, in far-away Mexico. Today they have completely disappeared as a tribal entity.

On the southeastern border of the present Republic of Panama dwelt the Chocoes, who are still numerous and extend from the Pacific coast northward to and even beyond the Atrato River. They formed a kind of buffer state between the Central and South American nations.

In the course of my work I had the opportunity of spending many weeks among representatives of the three groups still in existence—

Cavanillesia platanifolia, THE CUIPO-TREE

The two vertical dark lines are termite tunnels, showing that not even these giants of the tropical forest are safe from the attacks of the destructive white ant. The boy at the left is the author's son and companion.

THE TREE LIMBS ARE ALL STRIKINGLY GROWING IN ONE DIRECTION (P. 70)

that is to say, the Guaymies, the Cuna-Cuna, and the Chocoes.

THE GUAYMIES

Up in the forbidding mountains and valleys that form a background to the landscape for the traveler on the steamers plying between Panama and David dwell the mass of the present Guaymies, about 5,000 in number, in their homes scattered through savannas and forests. From the time of the conquest to the beginning of the past century, they have been more or less under the influence of Catholic missionaries, but have since been left to go back to most of their ancient customs and ways of living.

Among the few vestiges left of that transitory semi-civilized condition under religious discipline, perhaps the most conspicuous is the flowing gown of the women, tight at the neck and reaching down to the feet. In every aboriginal tribe committed to their guardianship the first care of the pious fathers seems to have been to create among those simple creatures not the sense of modesty which is innate among them, but a feeling of shame of their physical beauty.

This is why in countries with a constantly warm climate, and where the rugged topography, the predominance of brush and bush, and the multiplicity of rivers make necessary only the scantiest clothing, we often see the poor females moving awkwardly in their cumbrous imposed garments, under which, however, they still wear the primitive and more practical bark skirt. It is true that when there is no stranger near the gown is mostly discarded, and if a rainshower surprises a caravan on the trail the women quickly strip, wrap their togs in a large Calathea or Heliconia leaf, place the parcel in their load, and then continue on their way.

The men do likewise, and besides when they go on a hunting expedition they invariably abandon their trousers before starting on a run after some wild animal. This practice has been adopted by the other more civilized natives in some parts, and sometimes one discovers a whole collection of blue trousers hanging on the lower branches of some tree at the opening of a forest path. In this case the shirt that forms the only other part of the male wearing apparel is taken off and tied around the loins.

The Guaymies are usually not of a very prepossessing appearance. Their stature is rather variable and their bearing has not the stateliness that is often noticed among other Indians. The lips are usually thick, the nose is flat and broad, and the coarse black hair worn short (see page 83).

In the Guaymi culture, a woman ought first to be strong, healthy, and a good beast of burden and day-worker. The children, especially the little girls, also have frequently lovely faces, with a warm brown, velvety skin and beautiful eyes. When they reach the age of puberty their hair is cropped short and not allowed to grow again until the first baby is born. Maidenhood, however, is a short stage of life for the Guaymi women, who not infrequently become mothers before having reached their twelfth year.

Face painting is a common practice, restricted apparently neither by age nor sex, although the women adorn themselves thus only on great occasions. Black, red, and white are the favorite colors, the latter being obtained, as I have been told, by the use of an ordinary oil-paint, which the Guaymies obtain at Bocas del Toro. Little girls keep their faces clean, but boys under twelve were seen with broad black blotches, without definite outline, around their eyes.

In men the decoration is always more elaborate, and certain peculiarities in the patterns, as well as the exact repetition of these by distinct people, lead to the belief that they had formerly and may still have a signficance as a totemic or tribal emblem. The groundwork almost always consists of two black lines starting obliquely downward from between the eyes, so as to form on the face a broadly open Λ, the apex of which is on the nose ridge. These black lines are variously supplemented by white or red parallels, terminal appendages, and the coloring in pink, by means of anatto, of the outline of the lips, which then appear much thicker than they naturally are.

In certain communities the wealth of people is estimated by the number of their cattle. Among the Guaymies the number of wives is the standard. The role of these in the domestic economy is not, however, merely that of a toy, as among certain Oriental nations. They constitute the working capital of the family, and their way of courting the preference of their master is not through love, but toil. They are little more than mere beasts of burden.

The typical Guaymi dwelling is a round house, about eight meters in diameter, with a conical thatch roof. The bare ground constitutes the floor, and the fireplace is either in the middle or at the side. These houses are not always walled. When they are they have no windows, but two doors placed at the opposite ends of a secant to the circumference of the structure. The walls are made of erect sticks brought close together and tied with vines. On the north side plaster made of cow dung and clay is sometimes applied so as to afford a protection against the wind (see page 85).

A BUNCH OF FLOWERS OF *Gustavia superba*,
ABOUT ONE-SEVENTH OF THEIR NATURAL SIZE

TERMITE NESTS IN THE SAVANNAS NEAR AGUADULCE (VERAGUAS), PANAMA

They are built originally around the stem of some young tree, which soon disappears, while the solid, dolmen-like columns stand indefinitely against wind, rain, and drought.

Benches along the walls are used as beds, although at high altitudes, where the temperature is often very low at night, the resting place is on a light floor just under the roof. Large nets, hanging from the beams, are used in lieu of wardrobes and closets, and the tilling, fishing, and hunting implements, all of a primitive type except the guns, complete the house furnishings. Nowadays the kitchen crockery is mostly imported ware, the only exceptions teeing the large earthen jars used to keep the *chicha*, or corn-beer, and the calabashes, of universal use in the tropics.

Their dwellings are located either in the midst of the forests of the lower belt, in solitary clearings far apart, or in the high savannas. In the first instance they are always at some distance from the sea, as the Guaymies, forced back into the mountains by the Spanish invaders, have long since lost the art of navigation.

PROVISIONAL SUMMER ROOF, MADE OF THE LEAVES OF THE NATIVE ROYAL PALM
(*Attalea gomphococca*): NOTE THE LONG PALM LEAVES

These forest dwellers are of a quieter and more submissive disposition, though their daily contact with the stealthy and hidden animal life of the woods has made them more cunning and distrustful than their relatives in the savannas. These, living amidst rugged hills in a relatively cold climate, and enjoying day after day the magnificent panorama of the surrounding mountains and plains, framed in gray clouds and blue waters, are more energetic and open, and also proud of their undisputed independence.

THE CUNA-CUNA OR SAN BLAS INDIANS

According to historical records, confirmed by tradition and by a few local names, the Cuna-Cuna extended formerly as far as the valleys of the eastern reaches of the Chagres River, and covered both sides of the continental divide between the present Canal Zone and the bays of San Miguel and Atrato. In the course of the conquest they offered a steady and stubborn resistance, and they have been

EL BOQUETE, SUMMER RESORT OF THE PANAMANIANS, WITH THE
CLOUDED CHIRIQUI VOLCANO IN THE BACKGROUND (SEE PAGE 71)

gradually deprived of a large part of their former territory.

The history of the last four centuries shows not only many instances of their bloody struggle against the hated invader, but also proofs of their ability for political intrigue. During the piratical warfare of the buccaneers, or free-booters, the Cuna-Cuna were their constant allies against the Spaniards, because they well understood that while the latter had come to stay, the former had no idea of securing a permanent foothold in the Isthmus.

When in 1698 Patterson landed on the beach of Caledonia Bay with his small army of settlers, the Cuna-Cuna received him with open arms, readily ceded the required portion of their land, and were to the end the trusted and trusting allies of the luckless Scotchmen.

Today, after 200 years, the natives of the San Blas coast still keep in their heart a warm feeling not only for the latter, but for the British in general. The late Queen Victoria is revered among them almost as a divinity, and even vested by some with the attribute of immortality. Two or three times, indeed, during my short stay among them, I was asked the question: And Queen Victoria—how is she? And my assertion that she had been dead for several years was always received with the utmost incredulity.

THE CURIOUSLY SHAPED FLOWERS OF *Catasetum scurra*,
REDISCOVERED IN PANAMA BY MRS. H. H. ROUSSEAU (SEE PAGE 71)
The yellowish-green perianth is purple striated, with a delicately fringed labellum.

THE ANCIENT CRATER IS NOW A GRASSY PLAIN
SURROUNDED BY DENSELY WOODED HILLS (SEE PAGE 72)

Their diplomacy has been shown further in the course of recent events, when the secession of Panama was followed by the advent of the Americans in the Canal Zone, who from the beginning have been looked upon by the Indians as new and formidable conquerors, more dangerous to their race than the Spaniards of old. Such an impression, originating in reports from the Colombian side, could but be confirmed and intensified by the many men of Nárgana, Urgandi, and other places along the coast, who had repeatedly come to this country and stayed in it for longer or shorter intervals, thus becoming eye-witnesses of its might and irresistible power.

So the San Blas people were thoroughly awed, and, as they distrusted the capacity of little Panama to give them the protection they needed, they turned to their former masters, for whom they felt all at once a love and loyalty which years of involuntary and passive submission had not been able to foster.

The venerable chieftain Inanaquina undertook the long voyage to Bogota to put himself and his people under the protection of the Colombian government. He never reached the goal, however. His adviser and interpreter having died of smallpox at Honda, the frightened old man turned in his tracks and succumbed to the same disease in Cartagena.

THE TOP OF THE CHIRIQUI PEAK, THE HIGHEST POINT
IN THE REPUBLIC OF PANAMA, 11,000 FEET (SEE PAGE 72)

It was then that a serious blunder was made by the new regime at Panama. The hereditary successor of Inanaquina was his nephew, Inapaquina, and following the news of the former's demise, he was effectively proclaimed as such and acknowledged in most villages. The Panamanian government, however, ignoring the respected tradition, appointed as supreme authority on the whole coast Charlie Robinson, a native of Nárgana, who as a child and young man had spent many years in the United States and fulfilled perhaps better than any other one the desired conditions for the office, but who, in the eye of the Indians, had no right to it.

This resulted in a splitting of the community, the more conservative part of which from Playon Grande eastward, continued under Inapaquina and the Colombian flag, while the Mandinga Bay natives indifferently accepted the rule of Robinson. Thus inopportune intervention has resulted mainly in the awakening

AMONG THE GUAYMI MEN THE LIPS
ARE THICK, THE NOSE IS FLAT AND BROAD

A GUAYMI INDIAN (SEE PAGES 72, 74, AND 75)

THE LITTLE GUAYMI GIRLS OFTEN HAVE SWEET FACES AND BEAUTIFUL EYES

among the majority of the San Blas Indians of a warm feeling in favor of Colombia.

The often circulated reports of the difficulty of penetrating into the territory of the Cuna-Cuna are true only in part. The backwoods aborigines, in the valleys of the Bayano and Chucunaque rivers, have nourished to this day their hatred for all strangers, especially those of Spanish blood.

So they feel that isolation is their best policy, and it would not be safe for anybody to penetrate into their forests without a strong escort and continual watchfulness. Many instances of murders, some confirmed and others only suspected, are on record and even the natives of the San Blas coast are not a little afraid of their brothers of the mountains.

Of late, however, conditions seem to have bettered, owing to a more frequent mingling with the surrounding settlements. An African of La Palma, at the mouth of the Tuyra River, told me of his crossing, some time ago, from the latter place to Chepo, through the Chucunaque and Bayano territories, gathering rubber as he

GUAYMI HOUSE IN THE FOREST: NEAR BY IS A CLEARING, WHERE PLANTAINS, YAMS, CASSAVA, AND OTHER FOODSTUFFS ARE GROWN (PAGES 75 AND 77)

went along with his party. At the headwaters of the Cañaza River he and his companions were held up by the "bravos," who contented themselves with taking away the rubber and part of the equipment, and then let their prisoners go with the warning not to come again.

The narrative of that expedition was supplemented by the reflection of an old man among the hearers that 20 years ago none of the party would have come out alive.

Among the San Blas Indians, the exclusion of aliens is the result of well-founded political reasons. Their respected traditions are a long record of proud independence; they have maintained the purity of their race and enjoyed freely for hundreds of years every inch of their territory. They feel that the day other races acquire a foothold in their midst these privileges will become a thing of the past. This is why, without undue hostility to strangers, they discourage their incursions.

Their means of persuasion are adjusted to the importance of the intruder. They do not hesitate to shoot at any blacks of the near-by

THE CUNA-CUNA OR SAN BLAS INDIANS ARE OF SMALL STATURE: PANAMA

settlements poaching on their coconuts or other products; the trader or any occasional visitor is very seldom allowed to stay ashore at night; the adventurers who try to go prospecting into Indian territory are invariably caught and shipped back to the next Panamanian port.

To the war vessel anchoring close to their coast they send a polite request to leave, and when a high official of the Isthmian Canal Commission asked to buy the sand of Caledonia Bay, to be used in the building of the Gatun locks, he was courteously refused, with the following reply from the old chief: "He who made this sand made it for the Cuna-Cuna who live no longer, for those who are here today, and also for the ones to come. So it is not ours only and we could not sell it."

To judge by the density of the population in the few villages visited by the writer, the San Blas Cunas, who also call themselves Tule, aggregate eight to ten thousand on the stretch of coast between Punta Escribanos and Cape Tiburon. Excepting Bocas del Toro, no other part of the Panamanian littoral is so densely populated, and there is no more orderly community in the whole Republic.

It is a great mistake to consider these Indians as mere savages. At least one man in every ten has traveled extensively as a sailor and has seen more of the world than the average Panamanian.

Many have come to the United States or to Nova Scotia as children and have gone back

SAN BLAS (CUNA-CUNA, OR TULE) INDIANS OF SHIATINAKA
Note the heavy gold disks hanging from the ears of the man on the left (see pages 90, 92).

grown men, with a relatively high degree of education. English is generally spoken along the coast, even to a larger extent than Spanish. The commodities of San Blas life are an incongruous mixture of native products and imported goods.

Primitive ways are perpetuated by the women, who have not been allowed, as yet, to have even a glimpse of the outer world and are, although perhaps to a lesser degree than among the Guaymies, the drudges of all work. The remarkable facility with which the San Blas men return to their simple and secluded life after staying for years in a more civilized environment must be attributed largely to feminine influence.

Times, however, are fast changing. Elementary schools, open to little girls, have already been established at Nárgana, under the guidance of a Catholic priest, and it is apparent

that woman will soon turn out to be the progressive element of the coast of San Blas, as she is in most communities of Central America.

Besides being excellent sailors and fishermen, the San Blas Indians excel in agricultural pursuits. The whole coast, as well as the numerous islands of Mandinga Bay and farther east, are lined with extensive coconut-palm groves, of a variety remarkable for the superior quality and shape of the nuts. Vast areas of the forests are covered with the native ivory-nut palm and the larger growth abounds in balata or bully-trees.

The last three products—coconuts, ivory-nuts, and balata—which are sold or bartered either to local merchants or to trading schooners plying between the coast and the United States or New Brunswick and Nova Scotia, are the main sources of wealth of these

SAN BLAS WOMEN AND CHILDREN, PANAMA: EVEN THE SMALL
BABY GIRL HAS HER NOSE-RING DECORATION (SEE PAGE 93)

SAN BLAS WOMAN IN DAILY ATTIRE

natives, among whom money is never scarce and poverty an unknown thing. The staple crops for local consumption are raised in small clearings scattered through the forests of the interior and reached by water from the coast; besides most of the usual fruits of tropical America, these include plantains, corn, rice, cassava, yams, and some cacao.

The land belongs undivided to the community, so that any encroachment is considered as a public damage. Annual crops are seldom produced several years in succession on the same piece of ground, but once this is cleared and tilled it belongs to the individual or family who have done the work, until it returns to the public domain through voluntary abandonment.

THE VILLAGE OF PLAYON GRANDE, ON THE
SAN BLAS COAST, 85 MILES EAST OF THE PANAMA CANAL
The houses are about 150 x 50 feet and each shelters 16 to 20 families (see page 94).

Any cacao, orange, or other fruit-tree planted by hand becomes an hereditary possession, transmitted through the female line. I was unable to ascertain the traditional laws regulating the ownership of the cocoanut-palm plantations, but was led to understand that it is the same that obtains for any kind of fruit-tree as well as for plantain groves.

They do not seem to have any religious system, but there are indications of their holding to the notion of a superior being, the author of all things and the embodiment of goodness, and also of a bad spirit, governing all evil, whom they fear and revere more than the former. Their *lele*, or sorcerers, are at the same time the medicine men and the representatives of that genius of evil—a sensible combination—since they are supposed to have the power to check the harm caused by the latter.

At the time of the blossoming of the fruit-trees, and when the yearly seeds are trusted to the earth, invocations in the form of recitals are sung by the men, and possibly offerings made, to propitiate the evil genius and call the blessing of the kindly God. I succeeded in obtaining a part of the invocation referring to the cacao crop. It seems to consist of an enumeration made to the *lele* of the several varieties of the cacaopods, and of an appeal to a being personified by the ever-traveling sun.

The San Blas Indians are of small stature, with the body unusually long and broad-chested and the limbs short. The head is round and large and cheek bones very high, the nose long and often aquiline. The skin is dark reddish brown in the men, a few shades lighter in women. The hair is jet-black and as a rule cropped short, though a few of the girls wear it rather long, and the men have sometimes the whole mass of it cut straight, or bobbed, at the neck. Most women have remarkably fine white teeth.

Polygamy is allowed, but seldom practiced nowadays.

As a result of their frequent intercourse with the outside world, the San Blas men have adopted rather ordinary garb, reducing it to the simplicity required by the warm climate. Their native hats are peculiar in having the form much smaller than the head of the wearer, so that they are kept in place only by the stiff, short hairs acting as a sort of clinching spring.

Many men wear hanging from their ears large gold disks, often of the size and thickness of a $20 gold-piece. They are reticent as to the origin of the metal. In old times they probably obtained it by washing the sand of the rivers,

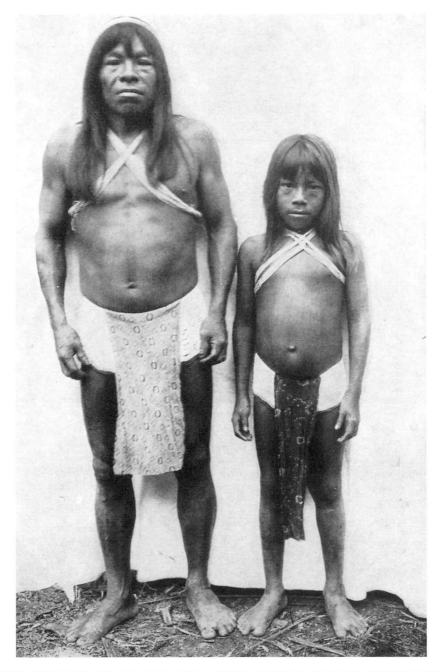

THE CHOCOES OF PANAMA ARE A FINE LOOKING AND HEALTHY RACE:
CHIEF DON CARLOS AND HIS SON (SEE PAGES 94–97)

CHIEF DON CARLOS' (LADY)

several of which are said to be auriferous, but at present they very likely use for their personal adornment American and English treasure, having it modified to suit their taste by the native gold and silversmiths established in almost every village (see page 87).

The custom of face-painting is rapidly disappearing. At one of the villages some boys were seen wearing a single blue line along the ridge of their noses, and the *lele*, or medicine man, of Shiatinaka had evidently rouge (anatto dye) on his cheeks. These were the only instances of this kind of ornamentation, formerly of much more general vogue. The Chucunaque and Bayano Indians, who, their scant

clouts excepted, dispense with clothes, are reported to paint their whole body jet black before starting on their hunting or fishing expeditions.

For every-day wear, the apparel of the Cuna women consists of a short skirt, red or blue, extending from the hips to the knees. The upper part of the body is covered with a kind of loose blouse, the sleeves of which do not reach the elbow. Over these two garments there comes a second skirt, reaching from the waist to the ankles.

Of course, with reference to skirts, it must be understood that the word is used only for convenience sake, not meaning the rather

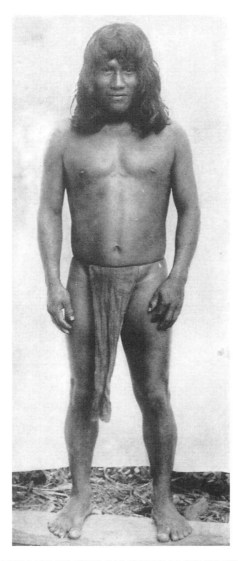

A CHOCO INDIAN MAN OF THE SAMBU VALLEY IN EVERY-DAY DRESS

complicated piece of civilized woman's raiment, but a single seamless piece of calico, not over four yards long, and rolled around the body.

The necks of the women are loaded with necklaces made of red, white, or blue beads, to which are added old Colombian silver coins.

They also wear, occasionally, in their ears gold rings or disks, these latter like those of the men, and in their noses always another ring of the same metal, which is seen even on suckling baby girls, and is never removed at death (see page 88).

At Armila an opportunity offered itself to study the gala wearing apparel of the chieftain's wife, who was evidently the village belle. She had on some sort of short "sheath skirt" of white materials, and a long coat made of the appliqué work which is a peculiar product of the Cuna-Cuna handicraft. Her head was covered with a bright bandana handkerchief.

Besides her ear-disk and nose-ring, she wore on each arm a broad cuff at the wrist and a narrower band at the elbow; her legs were incased each in three tight bands, bound together by three vertical strings. Through the broad intervals the muscles were bulging abnormally, showing that the bands had been placed long ago and never removed. All these latter ornaments were made of white beads sown closely together on a piece of strong canvas.

There seems to be much variation as to the size of the Cuna houses, but they all have the naked beaten ground as floor and a high gable roof.

The two islands at Nárgana are literally covered with large dwellings, about 150 feet long by 50 feet broad, the long ridge of the palm-covered roof being 30 to 40 feet from the ground (see photo, page 90). Directly under this ridge there is a large alley, running between two ranges of high pillars, which support the middle part of the structure. On each side other upright posts divide the space into square compartments, each of which is occupied apparently by a separate family. There are only two low doors at each end of the building, and the side walls are made of sticks tied together, as are all parts of the building, with mountain vines.

These houses are packed so close together that there is no space left between them. Each shelters from 16 to 20 families, the exact parental relations of which would be an interesting demographic study.

THE CHOCOES

"Les peuples heureux n'ont pas d'histoire!" While the history of the Cuna-Cuna could be written, at least for the post-Columbian period, by putting together the brief accounts of the Spanish chroniclers, the quaint narratives of old writers like Wafer and Dampier, and oral tradition still current among the people of the tribe, we know almost nothing of the Chocoes. They are seldom referred to in ancient records, and in modern times they have been visited by only one or two travelers, who have gathered but scant information. Our own visit among them was a short one, limited to the lower and middle part of the Sambu Valley, in the Panamanian section of southern Darien.

Never in our 25 years of tropical experience have we met with such a sunloving, bright and trusting people, living nearest to nature. They are several hundred in number and their dwellings are scattered along the meandrous Sambu and its main reaches, always at short distance, but never near enough to each other to form real villages. Like their houses, their small plantations are close to the river, but mostly far enough to escape the eye of the casual passer-by.

Dugouts drawn up on the beach and a narrow trail breaking the reed wall at the edge of the bank are the only visible signs of human presence, except at the morning hours and near sunset, when a crowd of women and children will be seen playing in the water, and the men, armed with their bows and long harpooned arrows, scrutinizing the deeper places for fish or looking for iguanas and crabs hidden in the holes of the banks.

Physically the Chocoes are a fine and healthy race. They are tall, as compared with

A CHOCO INDIAN OF THE SAMBU VALLEY: REPUBLIC OF PANAMA

His hair is tied with a pearl-embroidered band. Note necklace of coins

the Cuna-Cuna, well proportioned, and with a graceful bearing.

Both males and females have unusually fine white teeth, which they sometimes dye black by chewing the shoots of one of the numerous wild peppers growing in the forests. The skin is of a rich olive-brown color and, as usual, a little lighter in women and children. Though all go almost naked, they look fairer than the San Blas Cunas.

The hair is left by all to grow to its natural length, except in a few cases, in which the men have it cropped at the neck. It is coarse and not jet black, as reported of most Indians, but with a reddish hue, which is better noticed when the sun is playing through the thick mass.

In young children it decidedly turns at times to a blond color, the only difference from the Caucasian hair being the pronounced coarseness of the former. As there are no white people living within a radius of 50 miles, but only blacks, mulattoes, and zambos, this peculiarity cannot be explained by miscegenation and may therefore be considered as a racial feature of the Choco tribe.

In men the every-day dress consists of a scanty clout, made of a strip of red calico about

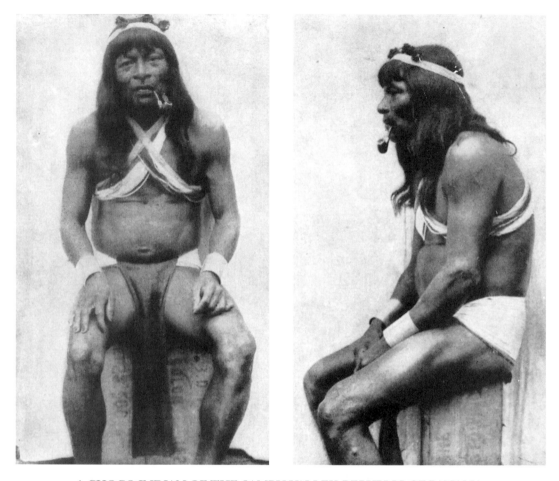

A CHOCO INDIAN OF THE SAMBU VALLEY, REPUBLIC OF PANAMA:
HIS HEAD IS ADORNED WITH BRIGHT FLOWERS OF THE FOREST:
NOTE THE BROAD SILVER CUFFS

one foot broad and five feet long. This clout is passed in front and back of the body over a string tied around the hips, the forward extremity being left longer and flowing like an apron. On feast days the string is replaced by a broad band of white beads. Around the neck and chest they wear thick cords of the same beads and on their wrists broad silver cuffs (see photo above). Hats are not used; the hair is

usually tied with a red ribbon and often adorned with the bright flowers of the forest.

The female outfit is not less simple, consisting of a piece of calico less than three feet wide and about nine feet long, wrapped around the lower part of the body and reaching a little below the knees. This is all, except that the neck is more or less loaded with beads or silver coins. Fondness for rings is, however, common

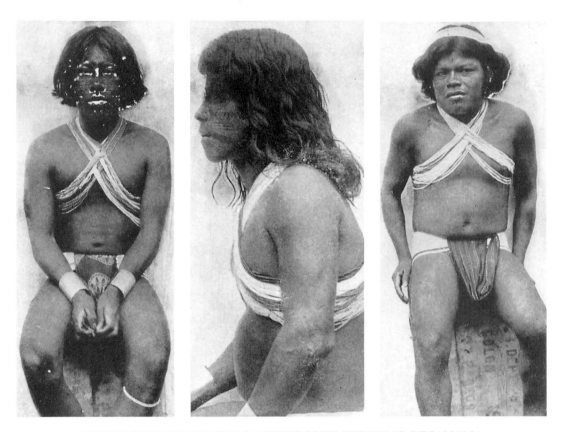

CHOCO INDIANS OF THE SAMBU VALLEY: REPUBLIC OF PANAMA

The fellow at the left has horizontal lines across the face, a pair of silver cuffs, and a string of beads on his left leg; the one at the right is unusually plump and fat. Note face-painting

to both sexes, and little children often wear earrings or pendants.

The scantiness of the clothing is remedied very effectually by face and body painting, in which black and red colors are used, the first exclusively for daily wear. At times men and women are painted black from the waist down; at other times it is the whole body or only the hands and feet, etc., all according to the day's fashion, as was explained by one of our guides. For feast days the paintings are an elaborate and artistic affair, consisting of elegantly drawn lines and patterns—red and black or simply black—which clothe the body as effectively as any costly dress.

From the above one might conclude that cleanliness and modesty are not the rule among the Chocoes. As a matter of fact, the first thing they do in the morning is to jump into the near-by river, and these ablutions are repeated several times in the course of the day.

The kitchen utensils are always thoroughly washed before using, and contrary to our former experience, their simple dishes, prepared

THE HOUSES OF THE CHOCOES ARE BUILT HIGH UP ON THE
RIVER BANK AND ARE SELDOM VISIBLE TO THE PASSING CANOES

mostly in our presence, looked almost always inviting. During our stay among these good people nothing was noticed that would hurt the most delicate sense of decency.

The Chocoes seem to be exclusively monogamist and both parents surround their babies with tender care, being mindful, however, to prepare them early for the hard and struggling 1ife ahead of them. Small bows and arrows, dexterously handled by tiny hands, are the favorite toys of the boys, while the girls spend more time in the water playing with miniature dugouts, washing, and swimming. The only dolls seen among them were imported ones, and they seemed to be as much in favor among grown women as among children. These latter go naked until they are about 5 years old, when the girls receive a large handkerchief to be used as a "paruma," or skirt, and the boys a strip of some old maternal dress for a "antia," or clout.

The houses of the Chocoes are built on a better plan, as far as hygiene and comfort are concerned, than those of either the Cuna-Cuna or the Guaymies. Placed high up on the river bank and seldom visible to the passing canoes, their structure is almost uniform, although the dimensions vary. That of one of the leading men of the Sambu Valley is rectangular and measures about 50 by 30 feet, the longest side facing the river.

The floor is raised eight feet from the ground and supported on each long side by a row of four palm posts, which extend through it and bear the weight of the roof. Trunks of the Iriartea palm, split open and flattened, form the flooring. The roof is palm-thatched and with four sheds, two of which correspond to the long sides of the houses and join at the top in a gable 12 feet long, while the two remaining ones at the ends of the building are triangular. There are no walls (see photo above).

Access to the floor is by means of a notched pole, which is turned over when the dogs are not wanted around, or also to indicate the absence of the family. The kitchen hearth is built at the corner least exposed to the prevailing wind, and consists of a square frame filled with clay, with a few loose stones on which to set the pots. Such a house has an ideal ventilation and affords at the same time a good shelter against rain and the excessive dampness of the soil.

At night the floor, which is kept scrupulously clean, is turned into a family bed. Long sticks are inserted between the slats and made to reach the ground below, and on these mosquito bars are hung. Bark mats form the bedding. The largest space is the parental nook, occupied also by the babies, while the elder girls and boys each have their own sleeping corner.

The Chocoes are very industrious. During the dry spells their life, of course, is an out-of-door one, planting and watching their crops, hunting, fishing, and canoeing. But when the heavy rains come they stay at home, weaving baskets of all kinds—a work in which the women are proficient—making ropes and hammocks, carving dishes, mortars, stools, and other objects out of tree trunks.

And right behind the house is the great forest. There the giant monkey-pot tree raises its crown 150 feet above the ground, extending its protecting branches over many other portly trees unknown today, but which may sooner or later find their way to the mills and shops of other nations. Under their shadowy tops high palms with elegant stems, ariza-trees whose trunks are hidden under hundreds of scarlet flowers, vines whose enlacing stems extend from branch to branch, and epiphytic plants that fill every available nook, all compete in luxuriance and beauty.

NORTH AMERICAN INDIANS

By Hon. George Shiras, 3rd

THE series of illustrations of different Indian types printed on the following pages of this number have been selected from the collection of Indian photographs by Mr. Edward S. Curtis, of Seattle. Mr. Curtis is a trained photographer, who some years ago determined to make a photographic record of the Indian tribes of the United States. He realized how rapidly the habits and character of such few tribes as remain on the continent are disappearing and the great value of photographs to the future generations who will have no opportunity of seeing these Indians. As the work progressed, the importance and largeness of the task as well as the expense of the undertaking became more and more apparent, but Mr. Curtis continued the work for nine years unaided. Last year, however, he enlisted the coöperation of Mr. J. Pierpont Morgan, of New York, who is contributing a generous sum toward the field work in order that the series of photographs may be completed more rapidly and the whole work published. It is estimated that the field work will cost about $250,000. The following is quoted from the preface to the first volume which will be issued in September.

"It is the purpose of this series of volumes to give a complete record of all the tribes of North American Indians within the limits of the United States that are at the date of these studies (1898–1911) living in anything like a primitive condition.

"All phases of the Indian life are pictured—the Indians and their environment, the types of the old and young, their primitive home-structure, their handicrafts, their ceremonies, games, and customs—with an object, first to truth, then to art composition.

"In these illustrations there is no making of pictures for pictures' sake. Each must be what it purports to be. A Sioux must be a Sioux and an Apache an Apache; in fact, every picture must be an ethnographic record. Being photographs from life and nature, they show what exists, not what one in the artist's studio presumes might exist.

"It is not the purpose of these volumes to theorize on the probable origin of the Indian. This is what he is, not whence he came. The years of my life and the magnitude of the work preclude the possibility of going into the complete detail of many questions raised by the dif-

A ZUÑI GIRL

ferent tribes. However, it is possible to treat the life so fully as to show future generations broadly what each group was like."

The publication will consist of twenty volumes of text, accompanied with fifteen hundred full-page photogravures. Several of the photogravures in each volume will be hand-colored plates of ceremonial subjects.

Each volume will consist of about 350 pages, measuring 9½ x 12½ inches. The best imported hand-made paper will be used, one selected particularly for its lasting qualities.

As a supplement to the twenty volumes, there will be twenty portfolios, each containing

thirty-six of the large pictures, 12 x 16, or in the complete set there will be seven hundred and twenty large pictures and fifteen hundred of the small, making a grand total of twenty-two hundred and twenty, these all to be of the very best photogravure work.

Mr. Frederick Webb Hodge, of the Smithsonian Institution, and editor of the "American Anthropologist," is the editor of the work. President Theodore Roosevelt has written the "Foreword."

It is published in parts, each part being complete in itself, treating of certain tribes. Parts will be delivered as completed, the plan

HOPI LAND

being to publish an average of three a year and the work completed within seven years.

The first two volumes, which will appear in September, treat of the Apaches, Jicarillas, and Navahoes. Volume 2 will cover the many tribes in southwestern Arizona and in the Colorado, Gila, and Salt River valleys. The different Sioux tribes of North and South Dakota will come next in order in volume 2, and volume 4 will treat of the tribes of eastern Montana. The fifth volume will depict the tribes of western Montana and Idaho and the sixth the tribes of eastern Washington.

Other volumes will take up the Mission Indians of southern California, the aborigines of northern California and Oregon; those on the northern Pacific coast and Puget Sound and the coast Indians of Alaska and the Pacific coast. One will be devoted to the Hopis and one to the other different Pueblo tribes. There probably will be a volume on the Seminoles of Florida, and Canada will have, without doubt, one volume which will practically be what might be called a treatise on the "Wood Indians." The final volumes will take up the tribes in Oklahoma and Indian Territory.

HOPI CHILDREN

President Roosevelt has written the "Foreword" which follows:

"In Mr. Curtis we have both an artist and a trained observer, whose pictures are pictures, not merely photographs; whose work has far more than mere accuracy, because it is truthful. All serious students are to be congratulated because he is putting his work in permanent form; for our generation offers the last chance for doing what Mr. Curtis has done.

"The Indian as he has hitherto been is on the point of passing away. His life has been lived under conditions through which our own race passed so many ages ago that not a vestige of their memory remains. It would be a verita-ble calamity if a vivid and truthful record of these conditions were not kept. No one man alone could preserve such a record in complete form. Others have worked in the past, and are working in the present, to preserve parts of the record; but Mr. Curtis, because of the singular combination of qualities with which he has been blessed and because of his extraordinary success in making and using his opportunities, has been able to do what no other man ever has done; what, as far as we can see, no other man could do.

"He is an artist who works out of doors and not in the closet. He is a close observer, whose qualities of mind and body fit him to

HOPI MAIDEN

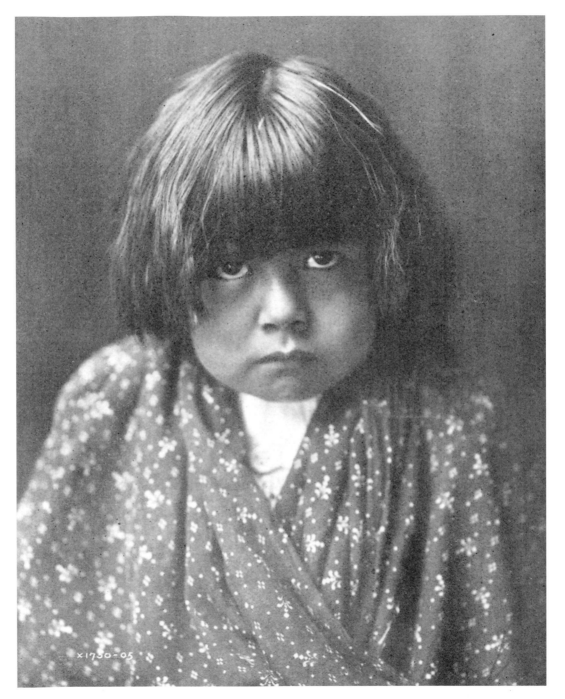

SOHOWA POQUI—SAN ILDEFONSO GIRL

A MOHAVE MOTHER

IN THE ORCHARD—SAN ILDEFONSO

A CROW YOUTH

AT THE POOL—CROW

APACHE MOTHER AND BABE

CHEDEH—APACHE

SON OF THE DESERT—NAVAHO

A NAVAHO

WATER CARRIERS—ACOMA

make his observations out in the field, sur-rounded by the wild life he commemorates. He has lived on intimate terms with many different tribes of the mountains and the plains. He knows them as they hunt, as they travel, as they go about their various avocations on the march and in the camp. He knows their medicine men and sorcerers, their chiefs and warriors, their young men and maidens. He has not only seen their vigorous outward existence, but has caught glimpses, such as few white men ever catch, into that strange spiritual and mental life of theirs, from whose inner most recesses all white men are forever barred.

"Mr. Curtis in publishing this book is ren-dering a real and great service—a service not only to our own people, but to the world of scholarship everywhere."

George Bird Grinnell writes as follows:

"I have never seen pictures relating to Indians which, for fidelity to nature, combined with artistic feeling, can compare with these pictures by Curtis. Today they are of high scientific and artistic value. What will they be a hundred years from now, when the Indians shall have utterly vanished from the face of the earth? The pictures will show to the man of that day who and what were his predecessors in the land. They will tell how the Indian lived, what were his beliefs, how he carried himself in the various operations of life, and they will tell it as no word-picture could ever tell it. He who remembers the two or three plates in Jonathan Carver's 'Travels' or Bodmer's splendid illustrations in Maximillian's great work, cannot fail to realize how great a difference exists between a written and a pictured description.

"The pictures speak for themselves, and the artist who has made them is devoted to his work. To accomplish it he has exchanged ease, comfort, home life, for the hardest kind of work, frequent and long-continued separation from his family, the wearing toil of travel through difficult regions, and finally the heart-breaking struggle of winning over to his purpose primitive men, to whom ambition, time, and money mean nothing, but to whom a dream or a cloud in the sky, or a bird flying across the trail from the wrong direction, means much."

THE NORTH AMERICAN INDIAN

THE first two volumes of Mr. Edward S. Curtis' work on the "North American Indian" have appeared, Volume I describing the Apache and the Navaho, and Volume II the Pima, Papago, Mohave, Yuma, Maricopa, Walapai, and Apache Mohave. An advance announcement of this work was given in the July, 1907, number of this Magazine. Mr. Curtis, it will be remembered, is making an ethnological study and a photographic record of all Indians in the United States and Alaska still living in a primitive state. His illustrations are to appear in twenty quarto volumes, accompanied by twenty portfolios, each containing forty large photogravures. The work possesses great historical and ethnical value, for Mr. Curtis describes and pictures the Indians in their everyday life, showing their customs, their games, and ceremonial life in a complete detail never before attempted. The foreword is by President Roosevelt, while the work is edited by Mr. F. W. Hodge.

The Apaches, who at present number about 6,000, for the most part live in the White Mountain Reservation of Arizona. Though their number probably never exceeded 10,000, they were for many years the scourge of a large region in Arizona and New Mexico. The name "Apache" is one of the most notorious and widely-advertised of Indian names, but very little was known about the inner life and customs of the tribe until Mr. Curtis obtained the friendship of their elders, and was by them initiated into many of their traditions and ceremonies. He had the good luck of being in the Apache country when the new "messiah craze" was at its height in 1906, and gives an interesting account of the religious ecstacy of this primitive folk. At present many of the Apaches are working for the government on the great Salt River irrigation project in Arizona.

The Navahoes, who are also described in Volume I, next to the Sioux, are the largest Indian tribe in the United States. They are self-supporting, and own large flocks and herds. They have been the least affected by civilizing influences. Mr. Curtis calls the Navaho "the American Bedouin," and says he asks nothing of the government except to be unmolested in his pastoral life.

The nine tribes treated in Volume II reside within the limits of Arizona, but extend into

THE APACHE

CHIEF GARFIELD: JICARILLA—APACHE

JICARILLA— APACHE MAIDEN

NESJAJA HATALI: NAVAHO

LUZI: PAPAGO

the Mexican state of Sonora and into eastern California.

The Yuma and the Mohave, whose homes are on the banks of the mighty Colorado, are usually fine specimens physically, being large boned, strongly built, and clear skinned. Within a short distance of them, in the high altitudes, live the Walapai, of the same family. They are the direct opposite of the river Indians—hardy mountain types, physically and mentally quick of action, for their rugged mountain home has ever demanded of them a hard fight for existence. Adjoining them, in Cataract canyon of the Colorado, are the Havasupai, also of the Yuman family, whose surroundings are truly unique. Though they cultivate small patches in their canyon home, for subsistence they depend much upon the chase, and, like the Walapai, are a wiry mountain people. The Maricopa, another Yuman tribe, who have long lived in the valley of the Gila, exhibit the effect of their Colorado river origin, both in their physique.

The Pima from earliest tradition have dwelt within the Gila drainage in southern Arizona. From one point of view they are ideal people—industrious, keen of mind, friendly to civilization, and tractable.

These various tribes have been broadly termed with the Pueblos, the sedentary Indians of the Southwest. Most of them came early in direct contact with Spanish missionaries, whose ministrations they received in friendly spirit, yet after more than two centuries of zealous effort little has been accomplished toward substituting the religion of the white man for that of their fathers. True, many are professed adherents of the Christian faith, but only in rare instances has an Indian really abandoned his own gods. As a rule the extent of their Christianization has been their willingness to add another god to their pantheon.

The Pimas and Yumas and their allies were the builders of those wonderful monuments of the Southwest which indicate that a great population formerly lived there, and has since been dispersed.

It is very fortunate that a man like Mr. Curtis is able to make a historical record of the Indians before they have been obliterated.

FURTHER READING

Oliver La Farge, *A Pictoral History of the American Indian* (1974), is an outstanding reference volume. See any edition. This work has established itself as a comprehensive, authoritative, and thoroughly absorbing history of the Indians of North America from Columbus up to the present. Herman J. Viola, *After Columbus: The Smithsonian Chronicle of the North American Indians* (1990), is a masterful portrait of a people whose cherished traditions endured a mighty upheaval. William C. Sturtevant, *The Handbook of North American Indians* (1978–1999), is another indispensable multivolume source that explains the history, culture and customs of the indigenous people of North America. See also Alvin M. Josephy Jr., *500 Nations: An Illustrated History of North American Indians* (1998).

INDEX

CONTRIBUTORS

General Editor FRED L. ISRAEL is an award-winning historian. He received the Scribe's Award from the American Bar Association for his work on the Chelsea House series *The Justices of the United States Supreme Court*. A specialist in American history, he was general editor for Chelsea's *1897 Sears Roebuck Catalog*. Dr. Israel has also worked in association with Arthur M. Schlesinger, jr. on many projects, including *The History of the U.S. Presidential Elections* and *The History of U.S. Political Parties*. He is senior consulting editor on the Chelsea House series *Looking into the Past: People, Places, and Customs*, which examines past traditions, customs, and cultures of various nations.

Senior Consulting Editor ARTHUR M. SCHLESINGER, JR. is the pre-eminent American historian of our time. He won the Pulitzer Prize for his book *The Age of Jackson* (1945), and again for *A Thousand Days* (1965). This chronicle of the Kennedy Administration also won a National Book Award. He has written many other books, including a multi-volume series, *The Age of Roosevelt*. Professor Schlesinger is the Albert Schweitzer Professor of the Humanities at the City University of New York, and has been involved in several other Chelsea House projects, including the *American Statesmen* series of biographies on the most prominent figures of early American history.